Hired 'Right'

Out of College

From Classes to Career
A Step-by-Step Guide to Discovering
the Career You Were Born to Pursue

Garrett Miller

Editor
Marilyn Gasior, Ed.D.

Content Editor
Victor B. Miller IV, MBA

First published by Dog Ear Publishing
4010 W. 86th Street, Ste H
Indianapolis, IN 46268
www.dogearpublishing.net

ISBN: 978-1-4575-1136-3

This book is printed on acid-free paper.

Printed in the United States of America

To all who are listening for the call...

...and

To Harrison, Davis, and Kathryn, who I trust will soon be engaged in the discovery process: that they may hear the call and invest their gifts and talents profitably.

What readers are saying about 'Right'

Hired 'Right' gets everyone asking the right questions to enable students to tackle the critically important process of discovering what they are designed to become. Everyone has a calling and this outstanding book helps students hear the call while providing practical ideas on how to answer the call. A must read for students and parents!
**John G. Miller — Author of *QBQ!*, *Flipping the Switch*,
Outstanding!, and *Parenting the QBQ Way.***

With helpful insights and rich advice, *Hired 'Right' Out of College* addresses the dilemma every college student faces by reconstructing the vague dream of success into a pursuit defined by small manageable steps.
Brittany Rhodes — UC Berkeley 2014

Garrett Miller hit the nail on the head with *Hired 'Right' Out of College*. This is the perfect book to guide students into fulfilling careers.
This book is a must read for all career counseling personnel, academic advisors, college students, high school seniors and parents. Our college advising office will begin to assist students with the "discovery process" using the tools and examples outlined in this book. Thank you Garrett. *Hired 'Right' Out of College* will be a welcome contribution to our students' future success in their careers. "AEIOU"!
**Shari Goldstein — Assistant Director Pre-Health Professions –
Florida Atlantic University**

Garrett Miller speaks directly and engagingly to his audiences (young adults beginning or completing their college years and their concerned parents!) about taking ownership of one's employment prospects and the best means of preparing to be hired. He urges each reader to engage in a candid assessment of one's own assets and liabilities (gifts, talents, affinities, or the lack thereof) and to follow a plan for personal development that leads eventually to being hired 'right' out of college. His advice is well worth heeding.

D. Bruce Lockerbie — Chairman/Founder, Paideia Inc.; Author, Speaker, and Educator (formerly at The Stony Brook School, Long Island, New York).

I was delighted Garrett Miller allowed me the privilege to review a draft of his newest book. This book will resonate with every parent or prospective student who is faced with a significant college investment. The cost of a college education has risen to such astronomical heights that you can no longer party and/or skip your way through college and automatically expect to get a job upon graduation. High unemployment rates have made the job market extremely competitive, even for the best students.

I recommend two readings. Your first reading should occur as you contemplate your college tours and potential careers. Your second reading should occur during the first week of your freshman year. This will ensure you are refocused and repurposed – and are therefore likely to select the courses and activities which will maximize your total college experience. This book is also a must read for college career services and high school guidance staff.

The self-discovery process outlined in this book is essential. This book will help you to obtain the right *Experiences*, as well as understanding your *Inward Call* and the *Outward Call*. Many college students are exposed to little more than the required classes, a few friends, TV, Internet and socializing. As Garrett says, "This often produces a malnourished degree and a severe case of career indigestion."

This book will help you to rise above the rest and will help to send you on your way to a satisfying, rewarding life path during and after college.

Charles M. Smith, CPA, CPC, SPHR — Director, Human Capital Consulting, J.H. Cohn, LLP
Charley can be reached at cmsmith@jhcohn.com

I have been waiting for this book for over 30 years. In speaking with college students about their future I often have wished for a book like *Hired 'Right' Out of College* to give them. I see the great value of this book to help them know how to find the career they will enjoy and find fulfilling, and to come to that conclusion with confidence. This is a book I will give to every high school graduate and urge them to read often to course their college experience. Garrett Miller has provided great insight in his book; I highly recommend it.

Ronald Pearce — MAR, M. Div. — Pastor, Hackettstown, NJ

Hired 'Right' Out of College is exactly what is needed to guide parents and young adults in their college research and journey towards ultimate and "best fit" career choices. As the parent of two, a college sophomore and a high school junior, this book truly hit home for all of us.

By connecting the concepts from self-discovery to career choice, the author brings to life the importance of understanding talents and gifts and how they can best influence what happens after college by making the right choices now.

I was honored to be able to contribute the little bit I did to this wonderful gift. Thank you Garrett for making this complicated and not always successful journey into an easy to understand pathway to possibilities for our children, their parents, and the coaches they rely on.

**Diane Faust — Senior Director Fortune 40 and
mother of two college students**

In his book *Hired 'Right' Out of College*, Garrett Miller is masterful in providing young adults with a robust toolbox of options to determine their passion. This is no one size fits all book. There are many different options and data points suggested—all supported by a solid plan to make it a reality. What's more, he puts the reader at ease about the pressure of intuitively knowing what they want to do for the rest of their lives—because most young people don't!

College is stressful for parents and students alike. *'Right'* helped me to show my college student that it is perfectly normal to not know what he wants to do for life. Our busy lives have enough pressure, determining your passions and life goals shouldn't be one of them!

'Right' constructively reminded readers that determining a career choice takes time, a plan and a bit of effort. It's a choice and a commitment—but once completed—it makes the return on the investment of my college dollars and his time—much more favorable.

Beth Beasley — Senior Sales Strategy Manager

A must-read for any college student wishing to make the most of his college experience. I found the author really identifies with students and provides a practical, step-by-step process to help answer the questions about what to major in and what career is right for me. A handbook that you should keep under your pillow.

Caleb Thrasher — Grove City College, Class of 2015

This kind of guidance will benefit students who are about to enter college. The wisdom provided can help young adults find their God-given gifts and interests and help them hone in the career path that God has intended for them. A must read for high school seniors or directionally challenged college students!

Chris Wagner — Senior Project Engineer and father of two college students

Hired 'Right' is the perfect roadmap for students seeking to make the most of their college experience. It provides a step-by-step process that students can follow to identify their strengths, talents and the type of work that will bring them fulfillment and success.

Kathleen Jackson — Career Advisor, College of Business Administration, University of Rhode Island

I would recommend this book to all college students as it really gets at the root of self-assessment, career exploration and career pursuit.

I would love to hand this book to every student who walks through our doors... it can serve as a valuable resource and really complements what we're doing as career services professionals!

Erika A. Mayer — Assistant Director of Career Services

Table of Contents

Foreword

Dr. Jim Thrasher
Director of Career Services
Grove City College

Yogi Berra said, "If you don't know where you are going, you might wind up someplace else." Do you know where you are going? Do you know how to get there? What do you want to do for a living? Why do you want to do it? These are all excellent questions which a student must answer at some point in his academic career. If you've ever asked them, *Hired 'Right' Out of College* is for you! The sooner you answer such questions, the more likely you are to invest in the classes, experiences, and activities that suit you best.

For eighteen years, I have helped students navigate this crazy experience we call higher education. My passion as Director of Career Services here at Grove City College is watching students transform from insecure freshmen into focused, equipped, and confident young professionals. We were recently recognized by the Princeton Review Guide as the 12th best university/college career services office in the nation. I believe we received this honor because we have tried to shepherd our students in much the same way as the one Garrett advocates in *Hired 'Right.'*

When I heard the title *Hired 'Right' Out of College* for the first time, I immediately understood what this book is about. It is a book about helping students hear the call. The call is that inner voice that longs to be heard. Many haven't heard it, don't recognize it, or don't even know that it exists. After reading *'Right,'* you will hear it shouting, and its voice will help you focus in on what you were designed to be. By working through the discovery process, you will be equipped to make better career decisions: decisions based on evidence.

Hired 'Right' is unique because its appeal stretches from high school seniors to recent college graduates. Both will find excellent practical advice to help them get more out of their education. Garrett has done a great job of breaking down the complex into simple steps that all can implement. Each chapter is short and digestible. Each chapter contains simple, logical instruction, followed by practical suggestions, then tied together with an engaging story of a student much like yourself.

My disclaimer is that Garrett and I are friends; there is a deep, mutual respect for each other's callings. We met when he first began recruiting on our campus for a Fortune 50 corporation in 1999. Like many of our recruiters, Garrett quickly became a friend and resource to our office and students. I remember him sitting in our office three years ago and talking about this project. That day I watched him feverishly take notes as he interviewed the staff. I am grateful that we were able to play a small role in this book, and I am excited to have a resource as helpful and practical as 'Right' to recommend to you and to our students.

Yogi was correct: If you don't know where you are going, you will wind up somewhere else. 'Right' will help you get to where you should be going. It will help you enjoy a more focused and fulfilling college career. I know that students who read this will be better prepared to be hired 'right' out of college.

Preface

What do I want to do with my life? What do I want to study? If you have asked yourself these or similar questions, this book is for you! My goal is to help you discover the amazing talents, gifts, strengths, and abilities that you already possess. As you begin to discover and uncover these qualities, your classes and studies will have greater purpose, and you'll become more energized and focused. Each new discovery will help clarify what you have been designed to do.

Being hired 'right' out of college has a double meaning. The first meaning is finding a job quickly upon graduation; the second meaning is not just finding *a* job, but finding the *correct* job. If you work hard in what I call the discovery process, you will be better prepared to be hired quickly and appropriately upon graduating. I will address how you can choose a field of study, classes, and activities that will point you toward the right job: the right job for you.

I believe you are special. I don't mean *special* in the way your grandmother might when she pinches your cheeks and tells you, "You're special." I mean *special* in that you are uniquely equipped, gifted, and talented. Life, college, and the pursuit of a career will become more focused as you uncover and discover each gift, aptitude, and natural ability you possess. You'll begin to gravitate toward the major, concentration, activities, and eventually the occupation and career track that best suit your gifting. You'll invest time in the areas that matter most to you.

Some of you may currently be feeling pressure to choose a major or field of study or to make a career choice. Because the implications of these decisions loom large and the ramifications can be significant, this can be an unsettling time. Some of you have already committed to a course of study but doubt the wisdom of your choice. Perhaps you chose your major on an impulse or based your choice on feelings. How can you pick the right major? You need experiences in order to uncover and discover what you are good at and enjoy doing. The good news is that you may have more experiences than you realize, and you can use those to make choices that will help you make better, more informed career decisions.

Many students enter college with little understanding of what they would like to study or do for a career. Many will spend the next four to six years meandering in and out of classes and majors, hoping the final major they choose will lead to a fulfilling career. *Hired 'Right'* is an easy and logical read with each chapter containing instruction, followed by helpful questions and tasks, all knit together by a relevant case study.

Your high school and college years are loaded with clues and opportunities for self-discovery! These clues are going to help you make confident decisions about who you are and what you were made to do. Seize these opportunities! As you follow suggestions from this book and gain a better understanding of your gifts, new experiences will be like unwrapping gifts: some gifts you'll absolutely love and others will be, well, like another pair of socks. But excitement and anticipation accompanies each gift you unwrap! So let's get started. Rip the paper off your first gift; it's time…

CHAPTER 1

Be What You Should Be

Dream Correctly

*"Starting out to make money is the greatest
mistake in life. Do what you feel you have
a flair for doing, and if you are good enough
at it, the money will come."*

Greer Garson

One of the most puzzling statements parents or other adults have made to children is, "Oh, honey, you can be anything you want to be; just set your mind to it." Ouch. Think of the weight of those words. Many kids have set out on the path to achieve their dreams, only to realize it was never 'in the cards' for them or that they were ill equipped to achieve those particular dreams. That is a devastating revelation.

The fact is you may not be able to be anything you want to be because some of you are just not equipped to fulfill all your dreams. If you are 5'8 and 146 pounds and your dream is to play in the NBA, I'm confident that it's not going to happen. The goal of this book is to have you dream correctly and then begin to invest in the appropriate activities, experiences, and skill sets so that you can fulfill your dreams. Dreams should be based on your innate talents, so that you *can* become what you were gifted to be.

**Dream based on your talents, so that you
can become what you were gifted to be.**

Sound a little heavy? Let me lighten it up. I enjoy quoting movies. Sometimes there's a hint of reality in them. Here are two

1

examples: "Luke, it is your destiny" and "Become the king you were supposed to be." Recognize them? The first is from *Star Wars*, as Vader encourages his son Luke to follow him down his career path. Fortunately for the universe, Luke realizes his calling lies elsewhere. The second is from *The Lord of the Rings: The Return of the King*, as Aragorn is handed the re-forged sword and encouraged to take his rightful place as the King of Gondor. These scenes demonstrate that these characters were set apart for certain roles. All their lives, they were being groomed by leaders and events that would lead them to a destined position.

If Hollywood doesn't ring true, life is full of great examples of men and women who were perfectly suited for their place in history. Winston Churchill told his wife early on in World War II that he was the "man for the times." Think about the list you could compile of people you know who were just perfect for the role that they served. Would Abraham Lincoln be on your list? Babe Ruth, Nelson Mandela, Mother Theresa, Martin Luther King, Jr.? How about Captain Sully (Sully Sullenburger), who miraculously and successfully landed US Airways Flight 1549 on the Hudson River? How about your soccer coach, science teacher, or pastor? Look at your list; it's almost as if these individuals were somehow called to these positions. Hopefully you see my point: people are given gifts, talents, and abilities. When those gifts are invested wisely, the individual and society benefit.

You are in much the same position. No, you're not about to be dubbed a Jedi or King of Gondor, but you are on an exciting path to somewhere great. If you're reading this book, you are probably a student or the parent of a student in or close to the college years. The purpose of this book is to help each student figure out who he is supposed to be and why.

In the days before GPS, there were many times when I thought I was going in the right direction, only to realize after miles and miles of driving that I was wrong. This book will provide you with tools to point you in the right direction. If you can discover your gifts, talents, and aptitudes early, you can head "north" or "west" in whichever direction your calling lies. By doing this early, you can avoid years of wandering and frustration. A successful discovery process will also prevent needless debt incurred by a college career that was extended as you struggled to find the right direction.

In the pages that follow, not only are you going to discover your gifts, but you will learn how to listen to yourself and others to help you discover your calling. You'll learn how the AEIOU formula for success will help you identify your gifts and strengths so you can make better choices when investing your time.

The college years are an exciting time of change, discovery, decision-making, and growth. Some students are intimidated; some are ready to rush headlong, screaming, "Damn the Torpedoes"; and others are just along for the ride. After reading this book, you should be ready and able to squeeze every last ounce of discovery from your college years.

Dream:

1. **What are your dreams?**

2. **If you could work in any occupation you wanted, what would that be?**
    - Why?
    - What talents or skill sets are needed?
        - Do you possess those talents?
        - Can you acquire or learn them?
    - Are you equipped to succeed in that occupation?
    - What type of schooling will it take to achieve that goal?
    - What type of dedication is required?

3. **When you picture yourself in a job, what do you picture yourself doing?**
    - Do you see yourself content in this job? For how long?
    - Does this job lead to a career?

4. **How have your dreams changed over the years? Why have they changed?**

<u>Note:</u> Below is a list of terms I'll be using throughout the book. You'll notice that they have similar meanings but significant nuances.

Definitions:

Gifts:	A notable capacity, talent, or endowment.
Talents:	A capacity for achievement or success; ability.
Likes:	Activities in which you find joy and satisfaction.
Dislikes:	Activities in which you don't find joy or satisfaction.
Interests:	Activities, ideas, and concepts you are naturally drawn to.
Aptitudes:	A natural ability to do something well and a capacity to grow in that area.

4

Temperament: A person's emotional and psychological make-up, included are qualities such as patience, thoroughness, and savvy.

Drive: An inward desire to pursue a goal or objective.

Job: A means to an income.

Career: A purposeful pursuit of a long-term occupation. Often involves a commitment to training, study, and investment of time, energy, and emotion.

Calling: A strong inner impulse toward a particular course of action, especially when accompanied by conviction of divine influence.

CHAPTER 2

College Pays Off
A Great Place for Dreams to Come True

*"Progress always involves risk. You can't
steal second base with your foot on first."*
Frederick B. Wilcox

College is not the only place to begin realizing your dreams. Many will choose a path other than higher education and enjoy the fruits of their labors. You have chosen to begin your journey toward your dreams through a college education, yet find the prospects a bit intimidating. Rest assured that college is a wonderful place to dream and achieve your goals.

Are you unsure about what you want to study, maybe nervous that you'll choose the wrong major or career path? These concerns are perfectly normal, but with effort and insight you will be ready to address them. College won't be four years you'll have to survive; it will be four years of purpose and preparation. Your college journey will bring with it lifelong friends, amazing memories, a terrific education, and a marvelous discovery—your potential!

College is not a prerequisite for success. As mentioned, many individuals enter the discovery process and find their calling without ever setting foot on campus. However, I believe that college, if approached correctly, can be one of the best venues for dreaming, learning, growing, stretching, and self-discovery. The time and energy you put into the discovery process at college will be a wise personal investment which will pay great dividends. College is designed to help you discover your gifts, talents, likes, and dislikes—all of which help you find your calling in life.

Though there are substantial costs to attend college, college can be a great financial investment. According to the 2000 Census

Bureau[1], there is a big difference between the lifetime salaries of college graduates and high school graduates. The average lifetime earnings are $2.4 million for someone with a master's degree, $2.1 million for someone with a bachelor's degree, and $1.2 million for someone with only a high school diploma. Clearly the long-term benefit of acquiring your college degree is an excellent financial investment.

As with every investment, you must make wise choices and commit to executing the plan that delivers the highest return. If you do, you have every reason to believe that there will be a positive yield. Now, does the prospect of bettering yourself sound enticing? College may be just the place to do it!

---

[1] The 2010 data was not available at the time this book was printed.

Is This the Right Choice for Me?

1. **Why am I in college? Is it for me, my parents, or my friends?**

2. **Why did I choose this particular college?**

3. **Begin with the end in mind.**
   - What do I hope to get out of college?
   - What do I want to be able to do upon graduation?
   - How soon do I want to finish?

4. **Why did I choose this major or field of study?**
   - Did I choose this field of study due to the urging of friends?
   - Did I choose this major for my parents or family?
   - Did I choose this major because it is easier than others?
   - Did I choose this major for status or financial gain?
   - Did I choose this field of study based on experiences in life that have pointed me here?

5. **What will this major lead me to?**
   - Is that what I really want to do?
   - Do I see myself content in that career or field?

6. **Is that where my gifts will be best invested?**

Case Study
Meet Vanessa

Meet Vanessa. It's February of her sophomore year in college, and she is feeling a twinge of concern. She's not sure if she's in the right major, but feels like she's too far invested in her studies to change majors. She's not feeling fulfilled, and though she's doing well academically, she doesn't see herself working in her field of study. Over the last few months, these doubts and concerns have begun to crescendo until she feels trapped in the major she chose. As she heads to class, she looks around at hundreds of her classmates and wonders if any of them feel the same way. When she scans the quad, her gaze settles on the career services banner flapping in the breeze.

I wonder if they could help, she thinks. *Maybe I should stop in after class.*

CHAPTER 3

Be Realistic
Dream the Possible Dream

*"When you discover your mission, you will
feel its demand. It will fill you
with enthusiasm and a burning desire to get
to work on it."*

W. Clement Stone

Do you need proof that you may not be able to be anything you want to be? I'm a huge *American Idol* fan, and I just love the audition shows. The judges often pose the following question, "Do you think you can be the next American Idol?" Each contestant says, "Yes, I do." The judges reply, "All right then, off you go." The singing begins. In seconds, the judges are giggling, turning to one another with the words written clearly on their faces, "He can't be serious."

The judges fight off laughter, bewilderment, or both, and signal the contestant to stop singing. The excited contestant waits with anticipation for the words he knows he is going to hear: "It's three yeses; you're going to Hollywood, baby." But in a cruel twist of fate, those words never come. Instead, he hears words he can't believe. "It's three no's…"

The laughter on the set stops as everyone watches the contestant's expression turn from great anticipation to sadness or even anger. He can't believe the judges; these trained professionals can't see or hear how talented he is. He'll likely say, "You're wrong; my friends say I'm a fantastic singer." A judge may retort, "Well, they are all lying to you." The camera follows the contestant outside to film him breaking down and sobbing.

I remember hearing one of the judges say, "How could her friends do that to her? That person can't sing at all. She has a terrible voice."

We come back to these puzzling words of encouragement: "If you can dream it, you can do it!" or "Just set your mind to it and achieve it!" These can be misleading statements because not everyone is given the same set of skills and talents. We have seen on *American Idol* and many other reality shows that not everyone who wants to be the next singing sensation *can* be.

For me, the rush of *American Idol* happens when the Chris Daughtrys of the world step up and belt out forty-five seconds of beauty. I am awed at how effortlessly they can sing, awed by how clearly they possess the gift and talent to perform. Watch the judges' faces light up; they also know. I love those moments. I want you to have an *American Idol* moment as well—in college and ultimately in your job.

Here's the exciting news. Every person is gifted. You possess talents and skills that are waiting to be uncovered, discovered, and developed. When you discover and then focus in on these talents, you will enjoy a more fulfilling and successful educational experience. Put into practice the principles in this book, and you'll be better prepared to enter the workforce and enjoy a more successful and fulfilling career.

I want you to have an *American Idol* moment—at college and ultimately in your job.

You can't be anything you want to be, but you should be what you have been gifted to be. You have been set apart for success. Now you have to answer the profound question: "To do what?"

Become Engaged:

1. **Does your school have a career services office?**
    - Not all career services offices perform the same duties.
    - The involvement, services provided, and proficiency of a career service department can play an important role when choosing a college.
    - Depending on the breadth of services offered, you may need to supplement some of the activities yourself.

2. **Have you visited career services? What do they have to offer?**
    - Career counseling?
    - Aptitude assessments to help you identify your strengths?
    - A library of resources dealing with picking a major, career, job, internships?
    - Workshops on interviewing skills, résumé writing, how to write a cover letter, and other useful career-related skills?

3. **Do you know any of the career service office staff by name or at least by face? If not, perhaps you have not spent enough time there.**

4. **When should you first visit career services?**
    - Your first visit should be as a new freshman. Schedule an appointment with one of the counselors and ask how the best students interact with this office.
    - What advice do they provide for freshmen seeking to make the most out of their college experience?
    - What have the best-prepared seniors done to get themselves ready to meet the working world?

5. **Plan on stopping by the career service office several times a year.**

6. **If you are struggling to declare a major, the staff at career services may be able to provide resources and advice to help you make a wise choice.**

Case Study
Vanessa Is Thrown a Lifeline

Vanessa has an hour before her next class. She slows down as she approaches career services. She watches the front door of this mysterious office, looking for signs of life. She sees two students, each dressed for an interview, one leaving and one entering. A sharp sense of panic and inadequacy courses through her body. *I'm not ready to interview. I don't even like my major.*

She pauses at the door, knowing there are a hundred reasons to put this off until later. But a clap of thunder and the ensuing deluge compel her to push the door open.

"Good morning." Dianne Reines has been greeting students for the last sixteen years at the career services office. She has the look of an aunt bursting with sage advice.

Vanessa scans the room and notices several students. One is quietly reading near the full bookcases; two are tapping on keyboards against the back wall, and she almost walks into a counselor and student who are deep in conversation as they cross her path.

"Can I help you?"

"I don't know. Do I need an appointment? I'm not sure—what do students—is this open to sophomores?" Vanessa pauses. "Sorry, but what do you do here—exactly?"

Dianne chuckles. "I'm the receptionist and office coordinater. But I'm assuming you don't mean, 'What do I do here?', but rather, 'What do we do here at career services?'"

"Yes, sorry."

Dianne hands her a brochure and opens it, circling several of the most popular services. Vanessa's eyes grow wide.

"Career counseling. Could you please tell me about that?"

Perhaps sensing the desperation in Vanessa's voice, Dianne adds an extra measure of warmth. "This is one of our most popular services. It's an opportunity to sit down with one of our counselors and talk about a host of issues, including interviewing, job searches, and your future career."

"Job searches? Career?" Looking at the name tag, Vanessa confesses, "Ms. Reines, I don't even know if I'm in the right major."

"You've come to the right place; that's our specialty. Would you like to set up an appointment to speak with one of our counselors? Our first opening is next Tuesday at this same time."

"That would be great."

Vanessa thanks Dianne. After filling out a brief questionnaire, she slowly pushes open the door. The deluge has come and gone and provided some much-needed relief from the oppressive humidity. Vanessa feels as if she has been thrown a lifeline.

CHAPTER 4

Begin the Discovery Process
Experiences are Essential in the Discovery Process

*"No amount of study or learning will
make a man a leader
unless he has the natural qualities of one."*
Sir Archibald Wavell

"Study hard and get good grades… Oh, and keep out of trouble." With those words, we are shuffled off to college, some of the most challenging years of our lives. *That's it? That's our pep talk? I'm supposed to go to college and be all grown up in four or five years? Is that the best advice the world has to offer?*

I'm about to say something that's going to frustrate parents and puzzle students, but here it goes: college is not just about the grades. What a loaded statement! Let me quickly clarify. This is not an excuse to do poorly in school and say, "Don't worry folks, Garrett says I don't need to worry about my grades." No, sir. Grades are important, but they are not the most important outcome you will take with you from school. What you discover about yourself is school's most important outcome. When you find your interests, aptitudes, and gifts, the grades will follow.

Many students slog their way through four or five years of college, only to emerge asking, "What do I want to do with my life?" This is a great question to ask, but you need to begin thinking of that question much earlier. By asking and seeking to answer this question earlier, you will be more focused in your studies and activities. This focus will ultimately help you prepare to be hired 'right' out of college or help you make the right choice about post-graduate education.

I've spent over twenty years interviewing and providing career counseling for students. I started by working at the career services office at the college I attended. We had open appointments available for peer counseling. Each day, I'd have juniors and seniors sit down with

15

me and confess that they didn't know what they wanted to do. They would share their transcript with me as if to say, "I've done well in my classes. Now can you please help me figure out what I want to do for a career?" I was surprised. They were at the end of their college career, and they were not ready to enter the world they were about to meet.

College isn't about their grades or transcripts; it's about what they've learned about themselves. Sadly, most spent their years focused on classes, the social life, or a mixture of the two, but not on how these classes would translate to a career or further studies. In order to be hired 'right' out of college, you'll need to add a healthy dose of discovery into the equation.

A recent survey by the American Enterprise Institute[2] of over 1,400 schools showed that, on average, four-year colleges graduate only 53 percent of students within six years. Are you reading what I'm reading in these statistics? That means that 47 percent of the students either didn't graduate or needed *more* than six years to graduate. Why would it take so long for students to graduate?

Many factors contribute to these alarming statistics. Some of them are completely legitimate. Many students delay graduation because they are not ready to meet and enter the working world. This may take the form of additional classes, a double major, or too light a course load, which forces them into extending their schooling. Maybe the most significant reason for extended college stays are the students who change majors; they must take extra classes to meet the requirements of the new major, resulting in longer college careers.

According to one report conducted at a major University, 70 percent of students change majors at least once, 20 percent twice, and 10 percent three or more times during their stay at college. There is ample evidence[3] that students can switch their major several times in pursuit of their degree. Why do you think students change their majors so often? Could it be because they are struggling to find their niche? Students are trying to discover their strengths and interests in the classroom, yet something is missing.

---

[2] Frederick M. Hess, June 2009

[3] Students Change Majors Frequently, The Bona Venture, 1/25/08 by Amanda Ciavarri "Stephen Stahl, dean of the school arts and sciences, said, on average, half the students in arts and sciences switch their major."

College freshmen face major dilemma, msnbc.com. 11/29/05 by Gayle B. Ronan "It is little wonder 50 percent of those who do declare a major, change majors — with many doing so two and three times during their college years, according to Grupe."

When a student uses the classroom as her primary tool for identifying her strengths and interests, that method can have several shortcomings. One shortcoming is that a student may choose to enter or leave a field of study based solely on one or two classes. Furthermore, the quality of the professors may have a profound positive or negative impact on her opinion of the major or course of study. The most significant shortcoming is that classroom experiences often do not necessarily translate into life experiences. There are many students who excel in a field of study but find that the career awaiting them has little to do with what they experienced in the classroom. The addition of life experiences to the classroom is essential for more accurately discovering gifts and talents.

According to the Bureau of Labor Statistics, the average Generation Y employee (a.k.a. the Millennial generation, those born after 1980) while in his twenties, changes jobs every eighteen months. One contributing factor to this job hopping is that some of these employees are trying to discern their gifts by constantly trying on jobs to see which career finally resonates with them. These Gen Y statistics also suggest this generation has not spent enough time in the discovery process. The discovery process is the frame of mind you need to be in the day you enter your freshman year. Ideally, it begins in high school and continues throughout college.

If you have not officially entered the discovery process, I'd like you to begin today. What you need to do is spend time, energy, and effort in this process. It will pay off! Enter it now by living, doing, and engaging.

The great news is that this process can be a lot of fun. In it, you will perform exciting tasks, meet terrific people, and be challenged. You should be pushed out of your comfort zone; you will learn more about yourself than you thought possible. I encourage you to take the path of most resistance. It's where great discoveries occur. Can you handle the challenge?

I encourage you to take the path of most resistance. It's where great discoveries occur.

In order for the discovery process to be successful, you will need more than just your classes and grades. You need to add experiences to the equation.

The Discovery Process - A Personal Assessment:

1. **How are you spending your time?**
   - Use a program like <u>rescuetime.com</u> to assess how you are spending your time on the computer.
   - Think back on this past week. What did you do each day?
   - Ask yourself if what you were doing last week added to your knowledge base? Did last week's activities grow and challenge you? If not, you must reevaluate where you are investing your time.
   - Are you scheduling quiet time for reflection, daydreaming, and planning?
     - Resist the urge to always be busy or connected electronically.
     - Create "white space" (quiet time) in your days; it's essential.

2. **In what extracurricular activities are you involved?**
   - If you are not in any extracurricular activities, go to the office of student life and see what's available.
   - As you become involved, you'll meet like-minded students and faculty in groups and organizations. You'll develop strong bonds and friendships while expanding your all-important network that we'll talk about in Chapter 16: Don't Jump without a Net.
   - If you are involved, are you committed to the activity or are you just a casual participant? Think about committing.
   - Try a stretch activity. Volunteer for something that's outside your comfort zone. This is the time of life and the environment in which to stretch. Go for it. You just might be surprised.
   - Look for activities where you might receive training.
     - A good rule of thumb: If you have an opportunity to learn new skills, jump at the chance. Learning from professionals is a great way to add to your skill sets.

3. Are you busy with a purpose?

- Are the activities you're engaged in growing you, exposing you to new skills, talents, and environments? Are you learning something about yourself and your aptitudes at the end of the activity?

Case Study
You've Come to the Right Place

Vanessa wakes up her smartphone by sweeping her finger across the screen. She checks the time again as her morning class draws to a close. The appointment at career services hovers over her like a visit to the dentist. She slowly shuffles out of class toward the quad. With the building in sight, she begins to second-guess herself. *Maybe I should just finish up this year and* then *see a counselor?*

Vanessa pauses as she approaches the door. Then she pushes it open.

Dianne looks up. "Hello, Vanessa. How was class? Have a seat. Mr. Simms will be right with you."

Vanessa wanders to the bookshelves and runs her fingers across the titles.

"Good morning, Vanessa," says a voice behind her.

Vanessa turns around to see Mr. Simms, Director of Career Services, approaching. He is tall and athletically built, with salt and pepper hair. He has a warm smile and an excitement in his voice that sparks a feeling of hope within her.

This might not be as bad as I thought.

"Is this your first visit to our office?" Mr. Simms asks.

Embarrassed, Vanessa replies, "I've been really busy and haven't had the time. But it's not like I didn't want to."

"Listen, we're just thrilled you're here. Would you like the full tour?"

"That's not necessary. I was just—"

"Think nothing of it. OK, you've met Dianne. You were standing in our waiting area and library. By the window are our four computers; that's our information superhighway. Those two offices are mine and my assistant's. That's the famous career service conference room. We're small and humble, but really powerful."

"Amen," says Dianne.

Vanessa finds herself giggling during the official tour. *OK, maybe this will be better than the dentist.*

"If you're all set, why don't we head over to the conference room and get started."

"I'm sorry it's taken me so long to get here," Vanessa says sheepishly.

"Not another word about it. You're actually ahead of the game. Many students wait even later in their academic career before they visit us, if they visit us at all. We're going to have some fun together and also learn a few practical insights that you'll find helpful." Mr. Simms leads Vanessa into the conference room and sits down. "So, Vanessa, what's on your mind? What brought you into our office?"

"I don't know where to begin. I'm not sure if I'm in the right major or studying the right subjects. I don't even know what I want to do when I graduate. Seeing students interviewing for jobs makes me anxious."

"Can I see your résumé?" asks Mr. Simms.

"Résumé?" exclaims Vanessa. "I'm supposed to have a résumé?"

"I can see the anxiety on your face. Yes, Vanessa, you are supposed to have a résumé, and I'll bet you do. Let's come back to that in a later session. Tell me. Do you like ice cream?"

"Do I like ice cream? Doesn't everyone?"

"I do. My favorite is cookies and cream. If you asked me what my second favorite flavor of ice cream is and I said, 'I've never tried another flavor,' what would you think?"

"I'd say, you're missing out on some of life's great treats. But I'd also question how you know cookies and cream is your favorite if you've never tried any others."

"Exactly. How can I know what I like and dislike, if I've never tried other flavors? In this office, our philosophy is to try many different flavors, or experiences, in the first few years of college. As you develop a clearer vision for your desired field of study, you'll return to the flavors, experiences, you enjoyed most."

"So, how does this relate to my anxieties?"

"Vanessa, the reason many students feel anxious about these huge questions is that they are often making monumental decisions based on little evidence and information. They have chosen a major, but are not sure why, or even if, they want to follow that career path. They have to try more flavors."

"More flavors, Mr. Simms?"

"Flavors, in these cases, are more experiences. The more experiences you have, the more likely you are to discover what you really want to do. It's as easy as AEIOU."

"AEIOU? The vowels?"

"Just as simple to remember, but far more powerful. I'll get to AEIOU later; it will all make sense. For now, let's talk about your favorite flavors."

"I see," says Vanessa slowly. "Mr. Simms, I'm in my sophomore year, and I'm really busy. I don't have a whole lot of spare time for more flavors—I mean experiences. I don't even know where to begin."

"Let's not get ahead of ourselves. The good news is that you've done much of the work already." Mr. Simms smiles and points toward the crowds crisscrossing the quad. "You're not alone, Vanessa. The great news is that you've come to the right place."

CHAPTER 5

Seek Feedback
The Willingness and Ability to Learn

"Listen humbly to advice given in love,
from experience,
and intended for your good."

Garrett Miller

"This is going to be some of the best news you're ever going to hear." The room goes silent as the *Idol* judge delivers his assessment of the vocal performance. You can see the excited anticipation in the contestant's face. "You're not a singer and you will never be a singer; this career is not right for you." The candidate's smile melts away, and the look of excitement is replaced with a look of despair.

"That can't be. I'm a great singer."

"No, you're not," says the judge.

"Yes, I am."

"No, you're not," repeats the judge.

"I've been singing all my life, and people tell me I'm a good singer."

"Then they are lying to you. Singing is not your thing—it's a no."

With that, the dejected contestant walks off without a golden ticket.

Some feel the judges on these programs are too abrupt; OK, maybe they can be at times. But what did the judge mean by "This could be the best news you're ever going to hear?" What could be helpful about hearing "You're not a singer" when singing is your dream?

Consider two true stories. Each is about a boy trying to get out of a dead-end town, one a steel town and the other a coal town. Both stories were made into movies. The first movie is titled *Rudy* (TriStar Pictures 1993). *Rudy* is an exciting story about a boy, Daniel Ruettiger, nicknamed Rudy, whose lifelong dream is to play Notre Dame Football. Everyone tells him that he is too small and can't do it. Well, Rudy is out to prove them wrong. He walks onto that practice field with more determination than any other player because he has to work harder to make up for his lack of size and strength. He has to have more heart to compensate for his lack of natural ability. Guess what? He makes the practice squad. He is a Notre Dame Football player, but he only plays on the practice squad—all four years.

Every day, he works as hard or harder than his teammates, and every week he continues on the practice squad. His coaches love him; his teammates love him. He is an inspiration to everyone he comes in contact with. It isn't until the last play of his last game of his senior year, with seconds left, that Rudy is placed into a real game. He finally gets to play as a true Notre Dame Football player. With the crowd chanting his name, he breaks through the offensive line to tackle the opposing quarterback. It's a sack! The crowd goes wild. The game ends. The crowd rushes the field and carries Rudy off the field as a hero.

There are many aspects about Rudy's character that make him a remarkable person, and there is something heartwarming about the story. But I'd like you to imagine that the camera is slowly pulling back to reveal the entire field. As the camera continues to pull back you see the stadium, next his senior year, and finally his college career. In front of you, you see Rudy's football career in a timeline. Now add up the hours that Rudy spent on and off the field training for football from his senior year in high school until the final play on the Norte Dame Field. Maybe thousands of hours. Rudy practiced thousands of hours for one play in the last game, in the last minutes of his senior year.

Rudy invested thousands of hours in talent that didn't exist. Though he was an above average player, he was never going to be big enough or fast enough. He didn't possess enough natural talent to make it in Notre Dame style football or in professional football. Let's suppose that instead, Rudy had invested those hours, those thousands of hours, into an area where he *did* possess natural talent and ability. If, for example, he had a real talent and a gift with numbers and finances, where might he be if the same efforts were poured into a career in finance?

Setting your mind on the *right* goal and working toward it might be the better decision.

Please don't misunderstand; setting your mind on a goal and striving toward it in the face of adversity is not necessarily a bad decision. Nor should you listen to every critic and give up on your dreams because of difficulties or naysayers. We all know of individuals who've been successful despite being told they couldn't do it. What I am saying is: setting your mind on the *right* goal and working toward it might be the better decision.

The second story made into a movie is titled *October Sky* (Universal Pictures 1999). A boy, Homer Hickam, is stuck in a mining town and, like Rudy, is trying to find his ticket out. Homer's father believes that the only kids who go to college are those who earn sports scholarships. His dad wants him to play football, but Homer knows he is not built for it and would never make it. Much to his father's disappointment, Homer follows his natural gifts and talents and pours himself into the "foolish" study of rocketry. His dad tells him to get his head out of the sky. People in his town say he can't do it and make fun of him. Homer listens to his internal desire and to his teacher who recognizes his natural gifts and encourages him. Eventually, despite significant struggle, Homer and his friends successfully launch real homemade rockets. In 1960, Homer enters the National Science Fair and wins a gold and a silver medal in the area of propulsion. After winning at the science fair, Homer is offered numerous college scholarships and eventually goes to Virginia Tech to study engineering. Homer becomes an aerospace engineer for NASA.

In Homer's case, the thousands of hours were invested in an area where he possessed a natural drive, aptitude, and talent. The talent blossomed, and the investment paid off.

Unfortunately, Rudy didn't have an *Idol* experience in his life, or at least one that he listened to. You see, judges on *Idol* are professionals; their profession is finding and developing talent. They have a good ear and an eye for talent. Yes, they can make mistakes, but they usually get it right. When an *Idol* judge says you don't have talent as a singer, you should listen to him. It doesn't mean you have to give up singing altogether, but it may be worth your time to see if your gifts lie elsewhere and pursue those. The *Idol* judge wasn't being rude when he said, "You'll never make it in this business." What he was saying is that you don't have the gifts to be a world-class singer, so invest your efforts elsewhere—do what you were made to do. If the contestant is humble and can step outside of the image he has of himself, he may save hundreds, or even thousands, of hours of effort placed in the wrong direction.

Getting and listening to good counsel is essential. No matter what you think of the *Idol* judges, we all need good honest critics in our lives to balance those who are telling us we can be anything in life we want to be.

A critic is sometimes defined as one who offers a value judgment or an interpretation. This term naturally has a negative connotation to it. Instead, let's approach our critics as valuable tools to our success. One of the essential tasks before you is to find trusted advisors, people who will be honest and forthright with you. This can be awkward at first but will be incredibly valuable throughout your college and professional career. There is a quality called humility[4] that we must possess in order to be successful. Humility is defined as the ability and willingness to be taught. If you are open to feedback and coaching, you will be far more successful in life than if you resist it or don't seek it.

Find trusted advisors, people who will be honest and forthright with you.

You will find that when you set out looking for feedback, many are willing to give you their opinions mixed with sage advice. Be prepared to sift. Remember, these are pieces of a big puzzle that, when placed together on the same table and connected, make a much clearer picture. When you hear people's vision of who they think you

---

[4] Humility is one of the four essential qualities described in my first book *Hire on a WHIM* (Dog Ear Press 2010)

should become or what you should do, remember to listen, take it in, and process it. Later, we are going to put all this information together. Fortunately for Chris Daughtry, when he heard a 'no' from *Idol* Judge Simon Cowell, he also heard two yeses from the other judges. Eventually millions of fans displayed their agreement with the other judges by purchasing his songs and albums.

I've already established that you are gifted, but in what? You have a knack, talent, and/or ability, one that comes naturally to you. Haven't found it yet? No worries; it's all part of the discovery process which will unfold in the coming chapters. I'm going to help you find that certain something so that you can invest your time wisely. This will help you make the most of your college career, so that you will be ready to be hired 'right' out of college in the right field.

For starters, there are great self-assessment tools to help you begin to identify some of your talents, skills, and abilities. Many high schools offer these. Did you take one when you were in high school? Try and find the results; they may provide clues to help in your decision-making. These assessments have their limitations, and none are the Holy Grail, but they can provide valuable information in your search. Consider them one piece of the puzzle. Take a look at a few:

Aptitude Assessments: These are standardized tests designed to measure the ability of a person to develop skills or acquire knowledge.
- ASVAB is a military aptitude assessment offered to anyone old enough to enlist. http://www.official-asvab.com/

Skills/Strength Assessments: These assessments help to identify a person's skills and natural strengths. The results are usually accompanied by an in-depth analysis and commentary of your results.
- http://www.strengthsfinder.com/113647/Homepage.aspx

Personality Assessments: These assessments help identify your personality type and then suggest a type of work or work environment in which you might succeed.
- http://www.myersbriggs.org/
- DISC® profiling

As you become more aware of your gifts and talents, consider this graph as you analyze all the pieces you have spread out before you. You'll notice that it is not enough to have an ability or skill. You will also want to find joy and satisfaction in the use of your gifts. Likewise, it is not enough to find great joy in an activity; you also have to perform it well. For example, I might love to sing, but I may not have a particularly good voice (high joy, low ability). Or I might have an amazing voice but not find much joy at the prospect of singing for a living (low joy, high ability). When you possess a particular ability *and* you find joy in the use of that ability, you are heading in the *right* direction.

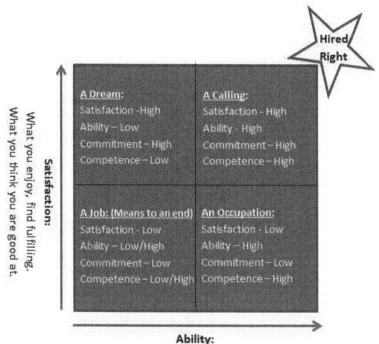

Find a Critic You Can Trust:

1. **Choose your critics carefully:**
   - Seek out individuals who are respected or come recommended by others in the profession or field of interest.
   - Find individuals who do not only criticize, but also offer helpful advice.
   - Seek out those who would have your best interests at heart.
   - Look for professionals who are also teachers and who communicate well.
   - If your critic sees promise and talent, look to nurture the relationship. Your critic may become a mentor.

2. **Find successful individuals in a profession or trade in which you are interested and have them evaluate your skill sets and natural abilities.**
   - Ask personnel from your career services office for names of individuals who are working in your field of interest.
   - Ask people working in the field if they can, and would be willing to, evaluate your work. (Honesty and candor are needed.)
   - Develop a series of probing questions you consistently ask each individual, which will elicit clear and helpful answers.
   - Learn what it really takes to be successful in that profession or trade.
     - Are you willing to pay the price and put forth the effort needed to be successful?
   - Do you see yourself doing what they are doing?
   - Are there similarities between people you are interviewing and your personalities and gifting? These don't need to be the same, but you might notice similarities that are relevant for success.
   - Have others evaluate your skill set and natural abilities in your areas of interest.

3. **Questions to ask a mentor:**
   - College/Professional development
     - How was your major relevant to what you are doing now?
     - Which classes did you find most helpful or relevant?
     - Which professors gave the best advice?
   - Activities
     - What activities or hobbies helped hone important skills?
     - If you had a chance to develop three specific skills before you began your career, which skills would you have liked to develop (e.g., public speaking, writing, conflict resolution, planning, languages)?
   - Results
     - Do you enjoy what you are doing?
     - Do you see yourself staying in the field or profession?
   - Internal make-up
     - What skills, aptitudes, and temperament do you possess that have helped assure you that you have made the right career choice?
     - What success or satisfaction have you enjoyed that has helped assure you that you have made the right career choice?
   - Looking back
     - What would you have done differently?
     - What advice served you best?

Case Study
Beginning the Discovery Process

"You don't know where to start? Let's start at the very beginning; it's always a great place to start." Mr. Simms spins around, pulls a few papers off the printer, and slides them across to Vanessa. The top of the first sheet reads 'Discovery Worksheet.'

"Discovery Worksheet? You're giving me homework?"

"The discovery process is going to take some work. I never said it was going to be easy. The heavy lifting has to come from you. My role is to help you discover you." Mr. Simms evidently feels proud of those profound words and, smiling, sits back to let them sink in.

"I was hoping I could just take a thirty-minute test that would tell me what I'm good at or best fitted for. My roommate took one."

"Did she find it helpful?"

"It said she should be an accountant. Funny, she hates math. No, not particularly."

"Vanessa, those assessments are helpful, but they are only one piece of the puzzle. They will shed light and help confirm some of your insights, but they are not the final say."

Vanessa drops her shoulders in disappointment.

Mr. Simms reads off a few questions: "Who are you? What are your natural gifts? What do you enjoy doing? In what do you excel? In what do you find satisfaction? What do others see in you?" He looks up and taps the document. "These are all valuable pieces to this puzzle. This Discovery Worksheet is going to help uncover these important clues."

Vanessa flips through the sheets and looks over a few of the questions. "That's it? I was really hoping to leave here with some of my questions answered."

"You're leaving here with tools to help you answer those questions. I'll play a more active role later on, but for now, you need to lead. Please fill this out and meet me here same time next week."

"OK." Vanessa sighs.

"Vanessa, here's a visual: it's your Discovery Road Map. I've filled in the first box for you. You are here at the top. You see, each of us has a set of aptitudes which are expressed and best discovered in our experiences." Mr. Simms traces his fingers down the diagram. "In future meetings, we'll talk about each of these areas and fill out the map together."

Vanessa glances at the map. "Aptitudes and experiences?"

"Remember how I said the discovery process is as simple as AEIOU? We have just encountered the A and the E: Aptitudes and Experiences."

"Aptitudes: What I'm naturally good at, my gifts. Right?"

"Yes, that is your homework. Because we know that aptitudes are best expressed and discovered through experiences, I'm asking you to spend some quality time filling out the worksheet."

"Are you sure you can't just tell me what I'm supposed to do? I think that would be a lot easier," jokes Vanessa as they walk toward the door.

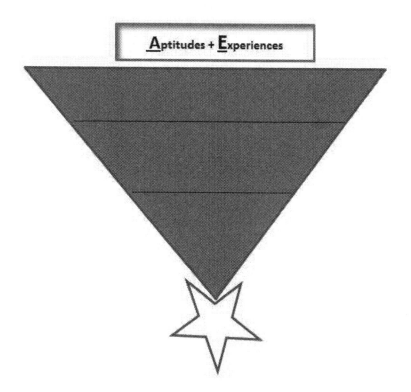

"Oh, why didn't you just ask?" Mr. Simms places his hand upon Vanessa's forehead, closes his eyes, and begins to hum.

"Get ready," says Dianne.

"Quiet, Dianne. You're breaking my concentration. Ah! I've got it." He opens his eyes. "You are destined to become a cruise director on a Caribbean ocean liner."

"Great. I get seasick when I walk by boats. I'll see if I can do any better." Vanessa gives a general wave to the office and heads out the door.

"You're off to a great start, Vanessa. Call me if you need me."

"Cruise director? I mean, really, Mr. Simms!" Dianne shakes her head.

Note: A Discovery Worksheet can be found in the back of this book.

CHAPTER 6

Plan or Pay the Price
Make Choices Based on Evidence

"Never desert your own line of talent.
Be what nature intended you for and you
will succeed."

Sydney Smith

Have you ever marveled at another person's gifts? Ever sit there and watch someone quickly compute a difficult problem, quickly fix the unfixable, sing a song without effort, or play a sport like he was born to? Have you caught yourself coveting that ability and wondering if you could do that? No need to wish anymore, because the fact is, while you may not have those particular gifts, you are gifted. Once you recognize your gifts, talents, likes, and dislikes, finding your place in this world becomes a whole lot easier. Once you have discovered your gifts, deciding what to major in, what classes to take, or what career to choose will be easier for you and ultimately more accurate.

So, how do you find, identify, and define your gifts?

Unfortunately, none of us came with an instruction manual. It would be great if we could right-click on our brain, scroll down to 'properties,' and see a list of gifts uniquely included with this model. But we can't. Sure, we have some idea of what we enjoy doing. But there is more to the discovery process than that, and if you do it right, the payoff is substantial.

So, what's the big deal about discovering our gifts? Why not just finish college, look back on what you enjoyed and were good at, survey the job landscape, and work in the area that seems best? This approach is what we call the trial-and-error method: one in which a student keeps trying different majors, careers, jobs, and bosses until he finally winds up in the right occupation. For some, this can take dozens of years. I know colleagues in their forties who are still looking for their place in the working world. Do you know classmates who've changed majors once, twice, maybe three times? If you answered yes, then you know people who may be struggling to find their niche.

Some people who suffer a midlife crisis are struggling with finding purpose and joy in their careers. They don't feel like they have found their niche; they've not yet found their calling. When someone is using his gifts, he feels a fulfillment. When he has not found his calling, he experiences frustration and an unsettled feeling. When someone has found his calling, is using his gifts appropriately, and is doing what he is designed to do, he will be more profitable to himself and to society.

Turnover is high among new college graduates because many are doing the discovery process after college.

The trial-and-error method is the most common but least efficient method for finding your way. When you use the trial-and-error method, you resemble a confused shopper who's looking for the right pair of shoes. Can you picture her? She has mountains of open shoe boxes piled around her and an exhausted and frustrated sales representative hoping she has finally found her beloved pair.

I've spoken to corporate recruiters who said that they no longer hire recent college graduates. When asked why, they tell me that new college graduates are too much of a risk. "I train them, and I lose them," said one VP from a Fortune 500 company. "They're not worth it."

Their experiences are consistent with the study I referred to earlier, which found that college graduates throughout their twenties change jobs every eighteen months. The estimates to train and 'onboard' someone until he or she is productive can range from $10,000-$75,000, depending on the complexity of a job[5]. If you are a business owner and it costs $20,000 to hire and train a new employee, how likely are you to hire someone who may change jobs in eighteen

---

[5] Most studies indicated replacement costs to be about 30 percent of the position's salary.

months? In a good economy, would you take the risk of hiring a new college graduate and hope you could beat the odds? How about in a difficult economy, when profits are down? How about when the unemployment rate is high and you have a lot of qualified, experienced professionals applying for the job? Would you take the risk? Turnover is high among new college graduates because many are doing the discovery process *after* college. Everybody wins when the hard work of discovery is performed before and during the college years.

A wise business owner might want to hire graduates after they have been in the workforce for three to five years, knowing that most of the discovery and job hopping is finished. Trial-and-error method is costly for you and costly for the employer. Nobody wins.

Experiment and learn about yourself during your college years—not in the post-graduate job market. Experimentation and learning should help you identify your gifts. Once you accurately identify your gifts, you can hone and confirm these through rewarding experiences. This process makes you more prepared and less of a risk for employers. That leads you to being hired 'right' out of college in the 'right' profession.

Experiment and learn about yourself during your college years—not in the post-graduate job market.

So when do you begin discovering your gifts? The good news is that you already have begun, if you have been paying attention.

The Discovery Process - A Professional Assessment:

1. **Take a skills assessment test.**
    *   Did you take one in high school, can you find the results?
    *   Your career service office may offer them. There are dozens of excellent assessments available online.
    *   See Chapter 5: Seek Feedback for examples of assessments.

2. **List and describe your personality/personality traits, list your skills, and describe your temperament.**
    *   Once you complete the assessments, review the results with a counselor or mentor.
    *   The results may provide clues and confirm thoughts and conclusions you've come to in the discovery process.

3. **Take a five-year agenda assessment.**
    *   Write down the jobs and activities in which you've participated since high school:
    *   What did you like about each job and/or activity?
    *   Were you passionate or driven about any aspect of the job or activity?
    *   What did you dislike about each of these?
    *   What were you naturally good at?
    *   What skills were you able to improve upon during the activity?
    *   What are your favorite and least favorite memories from each?
    *   Do you find yourself in similar roles in the activities, (e.g., coordinator, leader, encourager, teacher/trainer, supervisor)?
    *   What do your activities have in common? Do they consistently reflect a value system, work ethic, energy level, drive, or strength?
    *   Did you include the volunteer activities in which you participated? How about the clubs, groups at school, and religious organizations? Don't forget these. We'll visit this list again.

4. **Write down each of the bosses, supervisors, or mentors you've had.**
   - What did you like and dislike about them?
   - What type of leadership or management style did you thrive under?
   - What lessons did they teach you?
   - What advice did they have for you?
   - Did they provide any insights into your strengths, skills, drive, and aptitudes?
   - Did they provide a formal evaluation of your work?
     - Find and review their assessments, encouragements, and noted opportunities for improvement.

5. **Think of the type of skills and talents you've learned along the way. In what training classes have you participated?**
   - Were you exposed to formal/informal training over the years (e.g., CPR, résumé writing, display construction, project management)?
   - How have you been developing your skills and talents?

Are you finished already? Return to this list. As you remember details and additional items, keep adding to it.

Case Study
What Does This All Mean?

Vanessa returns to her room, throws her satchel in the corner, pulls out the worksheet, and flops on her bed. She flips through the sheets and lets out a long, frustrated breath as she reads the first statement. 'List the jobs you've held in the past five years.'

Vanessa chews on her pen, then scribbles down the waitress job she held over the summer. Then she adds the cafeteria job she held last semester. She taps on the paper and adds the lifeguard position she worked two years ago.

Finished, she proceeds to the next section. 'List the activities you've participated in.' She rolls her eyes and lies flat on her back, staring up at the ceiling in defeat. *How's this going to help?* She closes her eyes and thinks. *Varsity soccer, that's one.* She writes it down. *Choir and the Spanish club.* She adds those to the list. "Oh, I forgot I worked as a waitress for two months," she says aloud. With that, she swings her legs around and makes her way to the desk, clicks on the light and dives into the assignment with some energy.

An hour later, Vanessa is still filling out the packet, going back and forth from section to section as ideas, jobs, and events pop into her head. She looks at the time on her phone. *Where did the afternoon go?*

She stands up and looks at her Discovery Worksheet, proud that she has been able to list at least a few items under each question. *Now, what does this all mean?*

CHAPTER 7

Building Your Case
The Pursuit of Evidence

*"The most exciting phrase to hear in science,
the one that heralds the*

*most discoveries, is not 'Eureka!' [I found it!]
but 'That's funny.'"*

Isaac Asimov

In the classic movie *Back to the Future* (Universal Pictures 1985), Marty McFly somehow travels back in time and must ensure that his future mom and dad have their first kiss.

One of my favorite scenes is when George McFly is preparing to ask his future wife to the big dance. George's son, Marty, played by Michael J. Fox, has convinced George that her hand is his for the taking and all George must do is ask. So George approaches a table full of young women, slaps his hand on the table, glances at his notepad, and says, "You are—my density!" Her puzzled look forces George to reread his notes; he regains his composure and delivers the winning line: "You are my destiny!"

Destiny and fate are gigantic words. Destiny has been defined as the hidden power believed to control what will happen in the future. Fate has a similar meaning. Some students believe, *I'll just go to college, complete my coursework, and we'll see what happens during my senior year.* Hoping on the magical power of destiny or fate is not how one plans on finding one's niche in life. You must actively pursue the discovery of your gifts, talents, likes, and dislikes.

Hoping on the magical power of destiny or fate is not how one plans on finding one's niche in life.

Have you ever heard of the legal term *discovery*? It's the process in a lawsuit where each side begins to probe the other for clues and evidence to support each side's relative claims. Boxes of files may line a room. Thousands of different emails are printed off and organized, and witnesses are called in and deposed. It's a very exciting time and the *most* important time in the life of the case. If you don't have a successful discovery period, you're going to have a weak case. You don't win lawsuits with weak cases.

You too are building a case. You are in the discovery process at college. You're trying to find evidence and clues as to who you are and what your future occupation will be. This is a precedent-setting case for you. It will have a ripple effect for the rest of your life. Invest in this process and discover who you are and what you are going to do with your life.

For most college students, the question of what they want to do with the rest of their lives nags them for the first two or three years. Unfortunately for many, the nagging is successfully suppressed. It's only as that graduation date begins to approach that panic sets in. *Soon I'm going to leave the comfort of this college life and have to find a real job—an occupation that I will be in for the rest of my life!*

Remember the picture in Chapter 6: Plan or Pay the Price of the young shopper trying on shoes? She employed the trial-and-error approach when shopping for that perfectly fitting shoe. This method is not a very productive or efficient way to find the career that's going to fit you. There's a better way. You can do it right now; you don't have to wait to graduate. You can start at this very moment. Are you ready?

The first step in your discovery process occurs in the lecture hall and in your current courses. Resist the notion that your semesters and classes are just means to an end: graduation. It's easy to breeze through classes, end one semester, and begin the next. If you're not careful, valuable clues in your discovery could slip by unnoticed.

Interests and opinions can change over time. There were sub-jects, activities, and classes I thought I did not like earlier in life that I now enjoy. That is why it is so helpful to look at your grades, activities, and interests over the years. It helps you see patterns.

I also don't want to discourage you from pursuing something that you are not 'naturally' good at, especially if you have seen progress and growth in that area. Keep this book in its context. I am speaking of career and calling here. For example, I'm not a natural musician, but I tinker with piano and would really love to be able to sit down and play some of my favorite songs. Although I don't see myself as a singer/songwriter, I will continue to pursue piano because these types of interests and activities help round me out as a person.

The Discovery Process:

<u>Internal Discovery</u>

1. **Every great case begins with an excellent discovery process. It doesn't matter which year you are in your schooling. Start now by asking questions.**

2. **Which subjects are more or less appealing to you?**
   - Spend time reviewing your transcript class by class.
     - What did you like and dislike about each class?
     - Which classes were engaging and why?
     - Which classes/subjects were less appealing?
   - Ask others what they liked or disliked about each class. This may help spur on ideas and insights.
   - Write down what you've learned about yourself and what piqued your interest in each class.
   - Look at the grades you earned. Why did you earn the grades you did? Are the grades a reflection of your interest or natural draw to this subject?
   - Keep in mind that you may have disliked or liked a subject/class because of the professor or some circumstance surrounding it. Push yourself to determine if there was anything about the subject/class itself that appealed to you.

3. **Do the skills, aptitudes, and talents required to succeed in each subject/class provide you with insights into your innate gifts?**

<u>External Discovery</u>

1. **If you are interested in a particular subject or major, speak to alumni who have graduated in these areas and ask how their studies have applied to their career.**
   - What did they do with their major?
   - What have others done with that major?
   - What do they enjoy about their career track?

- Would they do anything different?
- Where do they see themselves in five years?
- Can they recommend someone else you can speak with who also graduated from that major?

Case Study
We've Got a Jumper Here

"Good morning, Vanessa," Dianne says, just a bit too chipper for a Monday.

"Hi Dianne, did you have a good weekend?"

"Sure did. What a beauty of a Sunday. Mr. Simms was hoping to see you."

"Hey, Vanessa, you came back! Glad I didn't scare you away," says Mr. Simms.

Vanessa holds up her completed packet with a smile. "I really didn't think I'd complete this. But I—enjoyed it—or let's just say I made good progress."

Mr. Simms takes the packet and flips through it. "Nice job. We've got a jumper here, Dianne."

"Jumper?" Vanessa asks.

"Someone who is committed. As in 'jumped in with both feet,'" explains Dianne.

"Vanessa, your hard work deserves to be recognized. Follow me to the conference room."

Smiling, Vanessa follows him. "What's the surprise?" She sits in front of the computer that Mr. Simms has waiting for her.

"This is an assessment designed to help us see where your gifts and strengths lie."

"How come we didn't do this first?"

"Ah, good question. Two reasons: First, this particular assessment is expensive for us to offer. Your completion of the form I gave you last week demonstrated your willingness to invest in the process and showed me that you are serious. Second, if these assessments are just taken at face value, they could be confusing because you might read too much into them or might misinterpret them. Therefore, we only like to offer these assessments to students who are committed and who will sit down with a counselor and review the results. When your results come back, we will be able to review them together. The results get added to the discovery process."

"All right, I'm sold. Where do I begin?"

Vanessa follows Mr. Simms' instructions and begins typing in her name. "I'm jumping."

CHAPTER 8

Listening for the Inward Call
Know Your Passions

"If you always do what interests you, at least one person will be pleased."

Katherine Hepburn's mother

The inward call is a fascinating subject! It's as if your inner wants, desires, talents, and skills are literally calling to you, begging or waiting to be discovered, understood, developed, and used. This is an extremely important voice, and you should listen to it.

You say you have never heard this voice before. I'm sure you have; you just didn't recognize it. How do you hear and listen to the inward call? Start by asking yourself such questions as: What do I enjoy doing? What am I good at? What do I find fulfillment in? What do I want to do?

Let's start with classwork. Do you enjoy a particular field of study? Maybe you enjoy a subject that others just don't get. For me, it was economics. Economics was complete torture for most in my class, but I loved it! When I say *loved it*, I mean it was fun. It made sense to me. Unfortunately, I had a very different experience with calculus. I remember the last conversation I had with my calculus professor. He said, "Mr. Miller, you have earned a 59.6 percent. I do not have the heart to fail you for four-tenths of a percent, so congratulations." After I jumped up with joy, I promised with a huge smile that I would never darken the door of a calculus class again.

Be assured that my love for economics and disdain for calculus were not the final say in what I would eventually do. Although I love discussing economics, I'm not an economist. I frequently work with math and calculations, but not at the calculus level. My love of business and why markets and consumers behave the way they do was born in Econ 101.

There's another wrinkle to my story. I started out as a chemical engineer, and the economics course was a requirement. Learn to embrace different subjects, even ones you don't think are relevant, because you just may fall in love. When given the opportunity to choose an elective, stretch. I had no prior exposure to the study of economics, yet this turned out to be the direction I would eventually take. I also received a C+ in Econ 101, so it was not that I possessed a particular academic prowess for the subject, but I did enjoy it.

If you are able, enroll in a variety of classes and enter each with an open mind; you just may uncover an aptitude, strength, and fondness for something new and exciting. Examine your latest transcript and walk through your classes one by one to see which topics and classes you excelled in. Make a note of those. Now do it again and ask yourself which classes you enjoyed and found most interesting. You might also retrieve your high school transcript and perform the same exercise. Do you see patterns? Are there relationships that you recognize? Pay attention; these may be valuable clues to your strengths, skills, and 'that voice.'

If you are able, enroll in a variety of classes and enter each with an open mind; you just may uncover an aptitude, strength, and fondness for something new and exciting.

I hope you can see the value of these exercises, which take a few minutes but could help save you dozens of years in searching. I remember taking another required course: a writing course. As a chemical engineer, I didn't think I needed a writing course. Looking back now, I feel that it was one of my favorite freshman courses, I loved the writing assignments, and twenty years later I find myself an author. I'm glad the writing class was a requirement and that I took the course seriously because I've enjoyed writing ever since.

You must be actively searching and listening to the voice—the inner call. In every situation, there may be opportunity for you to recognize or hear it. If you are paying attention, the inner voice will begin as a whisper and crescendo into a shout. Make sure you are engaged in the discovery process.

I love soccer. I played soccer all my life and was coaching soccer before I had children of my own. There's a process that occurs every season. During the first month of practice, I place players in different positions and watch them perform. At times, I was convinced certain players would be perfect at particular positions. But after seeing them practice and listening to their input, I realized that they were better suited to different positions. I arrived at the correct decision, not solely based on my initial instincts, but also with additional input. The additional input I needed in the case of my soccer team was to see my players in different drills, activities, and scenarios.

Can you apply this to your own situation? In order to hear the voice more clearly, you too will need to carefully and thoughtfully evaluate the different positions and experiences you have had.

In academia, the equivalent is being exposed to different subject matters and evaluating each course and field of study. I know there can be pressure to pick a major or field of study, but I happen to be a fan of the undeclared major. However, I do understand some colleges require incoming freshmen to declare a major. When students enter their freshman year undeclared or chose a liberal arts track, they wind up being exposed to a healthy array of classes. It's often by being exposed to different positions on the soccer field or classes that we find, and others see, our interests and strengths.

If you are paying attention, the inner voice will begin as a whisper and crescendo into a shout.

The questions regarding what you are good at and like to do extend outside of the classroom. By now, you should have finished evaluating your favorite classes and experiences. If your list of favorite classes and experiences is short, you need to get busy. The more experiences and the greater the variety, the more likely you are to discover, uncover, or confirm talents, skills, and interests. You must be involved and active in order to get the most out of the discovery process.

The question of the inward call is an important one. It does matter what you like and don't like to do. We tend to gravitate toward activities in which we naturally excel. Haven't found it yet? Then keep busy with a purpose and stay involved. The more activities and the greater variety, the more likely you are to encounter your gifts.

It is now time to translate the discovery process into the inward call. The questions and your answers in Chapter 6: Plan or Pay the Price and Chapter 7: Building Your Case should help you hear your inward call. What do you like to do? At what do you excel? Are there subjects and activities that you gravitate toward? Look at all the activities in which you have participated. Which ones did you enjoy most? Why? Which ones did you find most fulfilling, were you happiest performing? Which ones came easily? If they were difficult, which ones didn't you mind working hard to become better at? Listen, it's that voice again.

What type of activities do you naturally seek out? In what environments do you typically find yourself? Do you naturally find yourself in crowds, in small groups, or by yourself? Are you always reading books on history, sports, or politics? If you had the choice to spend the day doing anything, what would it be? What do you dream about?

Be careful not to confuse enjoying a particular activity with your inner call; you can be misled. For example, my very first job was pumping gas. I really enjoyed the work. If I hadn't been careful, I might have come to the conclusion that I had a particular gift in dispensing petroleum. Taking the time to further evaluate my experiences showed that what I really enjoyed about the job was interacting with people. I've always been very social. This job provided me with another avenue to talk, serve, and get to know people. If asked why I enjoyed my first job, my response would be, "I didn't necessarily enjoy pumping gas, but I did love the social aspect."

My point is that you should evaluate *why* you liked each activity. Was it for the activity itself or because you were in an environment that allowed you to exercise a particular skill or talent?

Listening to the Inward Call:

1. **Look again at your list of the activities that you made in Chapter 6: Plan or Pay the Price.**
    *   Make sure you've included sports, religious activities, hobbies, and clubs.
    *   Roughly rank them in order of "I loved doing this" to "Never again."
    *   What about each did you like and dislike?
    *   In which of these events were you stretched?
    *   What did you learn about yourself in each of these activities?
    *   Were you ever surprised? Did you ever enter into an activity with dread, only to be thankful that you did it?

2. **List the jobs you have held, both paid and unpaid, and ask the same questions as above.**

3. **Look to see if there are patterns about what you liked/disliked. Can you connect any dots?**
    *   Share these findings with someone who knows you well, talk about some of these experiences. What aptitudes do they see?

4. **Which of the activities and jobs were you passionate about? Which of these didn't feel like work?**
    *   When thinking about the types of activities that you were passionate about, take time to determine if it was really the job or the particular activity you enjoyed, or if it was the skill, talent, gift, or environment?

Case Study
Studying the Greatest Subject

Vanessa glances at her phone as she enters the last response. *That wasn't too painful.*

She spins around to see that she is in the room all by herself. She stands up, stretches audibly, and walks into the next room to find Dianne.

"All set?" Dianne asks.

"Yes, ma'am, all finished. Am I done for today?"

"I'll let Mr. Simms know you are finished. If you need to use the restrooms, they are down the hall. When you are set, you can go back to the conference room and wait. Mr. Simms will meet you there."

Vanessa freshens up and meets Mr. Simms in the conference room.

"Vanessa, I see you've been busy with a purpose. I've taken the time to read through your packet."

"With a purpose?"

"Yes, I love the fact that you've participated in a wide variety of jobs and activities. All this busyness is ideal for the discovery process. You are making great progress."

"No offense, Mr. Simms, but just for the record, I don't feel I'm any closer to knowing what I want to do than when we first met."

"But you are. Here's what I'm going to ask you to do. Take your packet, go back, and rank your activities and jobs from one to ten. One means 'I hated it' and ten means 'I loved it.'"

"That seems simple enough."

"Also, I'd like you to write briefly about what you enjoyed or didn't enjoy about each. For example: I enjoyed being outdoors; I loved managing a project; I felt in control; I enjoyed speaking in front of people. Those sorts of details. Make sense?

"Yeah, I guess. You know, Mr. Simms, I am taking eighteen credits this semester, so I do need time for my studies," Vanessa jokes.

"Ah, but you are studying. You are studying the greatest subject: you."

"Is it going to count toward my GPA?"

"You mean your Giftedness, Potential, and Aptitudes?"

"Did you just make that up?" Vanessa asks.

"Yeah, pretty good, huh?"

"Oh, brother," Dianne says.

Vanessa picks up her packet. "OK, I'll see you next week. I've got a lot to think about." With that, she stands up, thanks Mr. Simms, and gives Dianne a sheepish smile as if they were both in on a secret joke. "Bye."

Mr. Simms breaks the silence. "Dianne, sometimes I amaze myself."

"Really, Mr. Simms? Giftedness, Potential, and Aptitudes?"

"I know. Write that one down; we're going to want to save that."

CHAPTER 9

Be Busy with a Purpose
Get Involved

"Everyone is gifted—but some people never open their package."

Unknown

What's the difference between being busy and being busy with a purpose?

The difference is enormous and life-changing, so let's make sure we get it right. You can be busy[6] playing cards, sleeping, reading romance novels, watching sports or reality TV, playing video games, texting, hanging with friends, and surfing the net. In fact, I know kids who seem to be busy all the time with the above activities. What are they discovering about themselves? What opportunity are they giving for that inner voice to whisper, scream, and shout?

GET BUSY—WITH A *PURPOSE!*

Time is precious, and it's slipping by more quickly than you may think. Choose to invest your time so that you are always learning and putting yourself in the position to uncover, discover, and build your case. I know young adults who have invested hundreds of hours mastering video games or watching endless hours of TV and movies. I have no problem with playing games and watching TV, but discernment should be involved. After all, how much have you learned about yourself after you have played the third hour of a game or after you've watched your favorite rerun for the third time? As you carefully and thoughtfully evaluate your time, ask yourself, "What am

---

[6] The average college student spends 3.3 hours per day in educational related activities. Source: Bureau of Labor Statistics.

I learning or gaining from these activities that will benefit me in my discovery process?"

In order to be busy with a purpose while keeping your grades up, you'll need to practice good time management skills. Many colleges offer courses on how to schedule your time and help you prioritize activities. Learning these skills will serve you for the rest of your life.

Invest time wisely and the return will be incalculable!

College is an incredibly valuable time in your life—invest wisely and the return will be incalculable! I have surveyed over three dozen colleges and found that, according to the offices of student affairs, on average each campus offers over one hundred different activities and clubs in which students can participate. The SUNY system boasted over 3,750 student organization and activities. Each of these activities has the potential to introduce you to experiences that could help you discover your gifts and skills. These experiences can play a vital role in the discovery process. Make these years count by pouring yourself into purposeful activities.

Spend the time being busy with a purpose uncovering and discovering YOU.

I asked a friend, Noel Leuzarder, if she would share with me some of what she had learned in her four years as an active, invested, and engaged member of a student organization named SIFE (Students In Free Enterprise). Here is what she came up with:

How to:
- Create a professional looking document
- Lead by example
- Write concisely & professionally
- Develop a script
- Present to small and large groups
- Communicate well
- Describe statistics vs. results
- Be animated
- Make a good first impression
- Write a résumé
- Write letters of reference
- Use a teleprompter
- Interview both over the phone and in person
- Ask for and accept advice
- Be positive while being realistic
- Work with friends
- Develop self-confidence
- Develop a strong work ethic
- Channel adrenaline
- Overcome fear
- Network
- Maintain work/life balance
- Empower my peers
- Balance leader vs. managerial roles
- Seize opportunities that come my way
- Make wise, practical decisions, not emotional ones
- Eliminate an entitlement mentality
- Write a SWOT analysis
- Create viable business recommendations
- Perform business analytics
- Teach/instruct others
- Find a support system
- Find where I fit
- Perform benchmarking analysis
- Meet and be early for deadlines

How to:
- Interview on the radio
- Write press releases
- Manage time and scheduling
- Organize
- Become more responsible
- Respectfully rebuke, disagree, suggest, and correct
- Focus
- Multitask
- Anticipate and take action
- Work with people I like and don't like
- Be and work independently
- Work smart vs. work hard
- Relate to people older than me
- Brainstorm ideas
- Earn and gain respect
- Encourage others
- Deal with stress
- Accept rebuke or criticism, then listen and change
- Be light in darkness
- Work with PowerPoint
- Troubleshoot
- Test and push myself
- Substitute teach
- Create an annual report
- Create lesson plans
- Track inventory
- Sell items and ideas
- Create sales channels
- Apply for grants

The Importance of:
- Remembering small details
- Being slow to speak
- Finding joy in work
- Fixing mistakes I make
- Business etiquette
- Synergy and perseverance
- Having a hobby
- Modeling good behavior
- Creating, planning, & implementing
- Working outside my comfort zone
- Remaining ME under peer pressure

- Working efficiently & effectively
- Dedication
- Experiential vs. textbook learning
- Treating employees fairly
- Sticking to my word
- Showing appreciation
- Not being defensive
- Internal focus and control
- Asking questions all the time
- Being early vs. on-time or late
- Writing thank-you notes
- Avoiding negativity with a team
- A team's success rather than my own
- Surrounding myself with good examples
- Not allowing others to win by bringing me down
- Not bringing others down to bring myself up
- Taking the path of highest resistance and striving for excellence
- Presenting a problem and solution, never just the problem
- Getting to know people
- Being humble and avoiding pride
- Being open to constantly grow
- Expecting and anticipating to learn new things every day
- Never feeling 'I deserve,' instead feeling I must work and earn
- Using the gifts I discovered I had
- Keeping problems at home away from the workplace
- Putting myself second
- Creating a back-up plan and a back-up plan for the back-up plan
- Eye contact

This is what I call busy with a purpose. What skills are your activities exposing you to? Notice most of these skills being developed and nurtured will serve her for the rest of her personal and professional life. When you invest your time in the right activities, it is as if you are acquiring a *second* education.

Are You Just Busy or Busy With a Purpose?

In Chapter 4: Begin the Discovery Process, we spoke about keeping track of your time. Now let's evaluate what that looks like.

1. **Sign up for and attend a time management workshop on campus.**
   - If you can, explore some tips on time management online. There are great resources available.
   - Visit www.hired-right.com for some great time management resources.
   - For inspiration on using time wisely view this clip (http://www.youtube.com/watch?v=mF4vj5g7UUE) about the value of 86,400 seconds a day.

2. **Can you account for each hour of the day and then each week?**
   - Start with making a spreadsheet with the days across the top and the hours down the left side. You can break the time up into 30 or 15 minute blocks. The more specific the better.
   - Insert your classes in each day, allowing 15-30 minutes on either end for transition time. Now color code those.
   - Next place in your meal times and color code them.
   - Now it's time to fill out the rest of your schedule with a job, sports, extracurricular activities, study, social, reading, down time, quiet time, naps, phone, exercise, and anything else that occupies your time. Try to account for 90 percent of each day.
   - Commit to doing this for just one week, and then evaluate your time. If you felt this was valuable, continue to track your time.
   - This exercise is similar to looking online through your bank account activity or your credit card purchases. You are discovering how you are spending or investing your time.

3. **When you have completed a week, try to add up the time you have spent on your studies, work, activities, social, sleep, etc.**
   - How much time is unaccounted for? Be aware of this number.
   - Would you conclude that you have been busy with a purpose? Have you been involved in a variety of activities that are going to expose you to different opportunities to uncover and discover your gifts?
   - If you see that you are not spending enough time in the discovery process, head over to the student life office or find them online right now and add one activity to your list. The great news is that many of these activities wind up being social as well. Get involved, stay involved, and discover you.

<u>Note</u>: Hopefully you are actively engaged in the discovery process. If not, you may find yourself in the process *after* you graduate, which will be more difficult and painful.

Case Study
The Inward Call

Vanessa returns the following week with her completed assignment and waits in the conference room for Mr. Simms to join her.

"Vanessa, how's your GPA?" asks Mr. Simms as he sweeps into the room.

"My GPA?" Vanessa asks slowly, confused. "Oh, yeah, my GPA—Gifts, Potential, and Aptitudes. Just great, thanks. If ranking my activities means I'm closer to graduating your class, I'm doing better than I was last week."

"I don't know that anyone ever graduates his class, Vanessa," Dianne says.

"Now, ladies, this is serious business, no fooling around. Tell me, Vanessa, what did you discover?"

"Mr. Simms, I'll have to tell you that I was surprised by what I discovered."

"Discovered! Yes, now we are cookin'."

"Two things popped out at me. The first is that in my high school years I was involved in many musical events and activities."

"What do you mean?"

"Look here: choir, Madrigals, participation in three of my high school plays, singing in the church choir, playing in the marching band, performing in each of my school's talent nights, and singing lead for a cover band. Music, music, music. I don't think I was very diverse in my activities."

"That's an excellent pickup. Though I'm pleased that students like you are busy, you risk being lopsided." Mr. Simms spins the list toward him and looks at the activities. "This is much better than you might think. Let's talk about these."

Vanessa spends the next twenty-five minutes reviewing her list of activities, what she liked and disliked about each, and what she learned from them. Mr. Simms reviews the results from her assessment and helps her to see connections between what she finds and what the assessment reveals. They then focus on what she really enjoyed doing and what she found passion and satisfaction in.

"I've had friends suggest to me that maybe I should be in show business. Looking at all the entertaining I do, maybe I should consider it? What do you think?"

Mr. Simms sits quietly for a moment, tapping his pen on the table. "Vanessa, you've come across a very tricky area: the question of hobby vs. calling. I'm really glad you brought this up because many students have asked similar questions. I meet students that have amazing talents: students who are artists, singers, or musicians. They have more talent in their pinky then I'll ever have. Yet, though they continually hear accolades from family and friends, at some point they need to ask, 'Is this a hobby or is this a calling?' How they answer this question will have a dramatic impact on their choices."

"I never really saw it like that, but, sure, that makes sense. I mean, I can sing, but I don't really believe I have what it would take to be an accomplished singer. Frankly, Mr. Simms, I don't think I have the drive to be one either."

Mr. Simms smiles, clearly satisfied with Vanessa's progress in her discovery. "Vanessa, I love woodworking. When I have downtime, I can be found tinkering in my woodshop. Yet, even though I might be better than average, I wouldn't consider ever taking my hobby up as a trade. I've heard it said that the fastest way to hate a hobby is to do it for a living."

"That makes sense." Vanessa lets out a sigh. "I'm really glad we spoke about this. I've felt guilty about not at least considering the performing arts."

"I'm going to ask you to do some soul-searching. Do you dream about this particular interest constantly? Is this where your great passion lies? Is it practical, and is there harmony?"

"Harmony, Mr. Simms?"

"When I speak of harmony, I'm referring to all the pieces fitting together. But when I speak of practical, I'm asking what would it take? What level of talent would you need to possess to make a living from your particular hobby? Is that what you are looking for in a career?"

"Yeah, I've often thought about that." Vanessa takes a quiet moment and then looks up. "Mr. Simms, I sing for fun. I like singing in the choir at church and karaoke with my friends, but I don't really want that lifestyle."

"Great job. In the assessment you took last week, I don't recall the performing arts as one of the conclusions. Again *a* piece of the puzzle but one that seems to line up with what you have just expressed to me. Vanessa, sounds like you are really thinking through these difficult issues. You've just encountered the I."

"The I, Mr. Simms?"

"Yes. The A are your aptitudes and the E are your experiences in which you begin the discovery process. Now we have I."

"I'll bite. What does the I stand for?"

"I stands for the inward call: your internal motivation and drive; the internal confirmation that you enjoy a certain subject, activity, or interest. These are areas that you find joy and success in, which offer clues as to where your gifts, talents, and calling may lie."

"Now I see why you had me answer the questions about my experiences and activities. That was helpful. I'll continue to think about my experiences and what I enjoy and am good at."

"Great, Vanessa. I'll mention one additional thought. If you are still considering a career in the arts, consider performing an informational interview with a few professionals who have chosen that career path or areas of interest. Learn from them so that you can really put this decision to rest and then move on."

"That is a great idea. I need to do that."

"Let me ask you. It seems you were quite busy in high school but have not been as active here on campus. Any particular reason?"

Vanessa looks over her list again. "No, no reason. I guess I just fill my time with stuff. I know where you are going, Mr. Simms. You're going to say that I've been busy, but not busy with a purpose."

"You're quick, Vanessa, and an excellent student." Mr. Simms pulls out another version of the Discovery Road Map and places it in front of Vanessa. "You see, the strength of this triangle depends on your experiences. The more experiences and the greater the variety, the more accurate your road map. You, Vanessa, are off to a great start."

"At least I have something going for me. I see the left-hand side is the I we just discussed. I see you've also filled in the top two sections. I now understand why variety is important. What's the best way to get busy—with a purpose?"

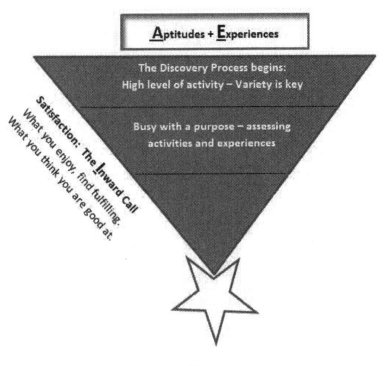

"Good question. Next door is the Dean of Student Affairs. Her name is Mrs. Bryan, and she's a good friend. Let her know that we spoke and where your interests lie. She'll help you find purposeful activities."

Vanessa glances in the direction Mr. Simms is pointing. "What should I do? There are probably a hundred different student activities."

"Yes, but now that you are looking to be busy with a purpose, you are going to examine each activity and see which ones will most benefit and interest you. These opportunities will expose you to new experiences to stretch you and put you into a position to confirm or challenge a talent, gift, or passion."

"I don't have time to take on more responsibilities. But I guess this is the opportunity to try playing in different positions, much like I do when I'm evaluating my soccer players."

"That's it. Not only playing in different positions, but also confirming the positions in which you excel. Try to recognize the positions and experiences which excite you, stir up an inner drive, and motivate you to invest more of your time and energy."

CHAPTER 10

Leverage Your Campus Experiences
Opportunities to Grow Everywhere You Look

*"Great thoughts reduced to practice
become great acts."*
William Hazlitt

While classes are not always fun and rewarding, the discovery process can be. If I've convinced you that you must be busy with a purpose, you might ask, "What exactly should I be busy doing?" College is the perfect time to identify your strengths and talents. Your years at college are the ultimate smorgasbord of experiences. Think of walking into an all-you-can-eat buffet with more food choices than you have ever seen; that's what college is like. Your mouth should be watering at the prospect of sampling as many casserole dishes as you can. Sadly, many students give a cursory look at the choices and settle into a routine that will expose them to little more than dorm life, required classes, a few friends, sitcoms, Internet activities, and a heavy helping of social events. This diet often produces a malnourished four-year degree and a severe case of career indigestion.

If you're not careful, a typical four year education might look like this:

Freshman year – A year of adjustment: too much time, not enough studying, but great success in developing a strong social network.

Sophomore year – Settling into a healthier routine: starting to dive deeper into my classes and major. Slight panic: I don't like my major; should I change or should I just stick it out?

Junior year – A more narrow social life, more serious about my studies. Now I'm committed to the career track. Or am I? Can I get a lifeline? I'd like to switch majors, but I'd have to stay another year to make up the required courses. Dad always said education is a great investment, so let's invest more. Panic! Realization that I'll be looking for a job before I know it, and I don't even know what I want to do. Wait. There's always graduate school— Yeah! I'm saved!

Senior year – I just discovered career services; I don't have a résumé or a clue as to what I want to do. Graduate school seems like a lot of work. Panic! I'll interview with several companies, hoping one will pick me up. Then I can begin to figure out what I want to do. I'd better fill out that graduate school application just in case.

Of course I jest; this may not describe you at all. But it does describe many who have gone before you. How can you plan for schooling more strategically?

Freshman year, you are in a new environment with what appears to be lots of extra time on your hands. Many quickly discover that they have between three and four hours of classes a day. Three to four hours a day—that's it? You think, *What in the world would I do with all that free time*? For the first few weeks, many will fall into a routine of getting up just before a morning of classes, returning for lunch, taking one more afternoon class, and having the rest of the day free. Maybe Frisbee on the quad, a pickup soccer game, dinner, a few of your favorite TV shows, rest, an hour or two of video games, a little homework, and then sleep. Wow, that was exhausting.

Sound ridiculous? That schedule was typical of many in my freshman class, myself included. Ironically, with all that time to study and master classes in my first semester, I managed to squeak out a GPA of just 2.1. The headline at this crime scene would read, "Student arrested for jaywalking through his first semester." I wasn't discovering *or* studying. Sadly, this is a familiar scene on campuses all across America.

Is there anything wrong with that schedule? No, just as there is nothing wrong with pizza and soda for dinner: a steady diet of both is unhealthy. If you buy into my belief that experiences help you determine who you are and what you are good at, a diet of our freshman's initial schedule will spell a good case of major (get it?) indigestion.

This diet becomes your comfort zone, and if you're not careful, this comfort zone can become quite narrow. Changing your environment and routine has amazing benefits. You can be served a wonderful four-course meal in a cold concrete warehouse and then be served the same meal on the veranda overlooking the Pacific Ocean, and you will have two very different experiences. In fact, the food will taste even better on the veranda. Striving toward variety will expose you to new events, social circles, environments, and experiences that will eventually have you engaged in the discovery process.

You need to be aware of comfort zones. Work. Yes, work at making changes and doing different things and going different places to participate in a variety of experiences. The problem with comfort zones is that they are, well, comfortable and easy. We slip into them as easily as we do an old pair of slippers. My suggestion is: plan, schedule, pursue variation, and savor each new experience.

With a little vision and thought, you can balance a healthy diet of social events with diving in and learning about yourself.

The experiences you have in college can be more valuable than the grades you earn. Don't get me wrong. The grades are important. Perform to the best of your ability. But it's the experiences that will grow you and mold you the most. Though classroom experiences are important, you often don't get a full understanding of your gifts in a lecture hall or textbook. It's through action, being involved, and doing that you come face to face with your gifts and talents. The greatest combination that you can employ while in college is being committed to your studies and being committed to the discovery process.

The greatest combination that you can employ while in college is being committed to your studies and being committed to the discovery process.

A great benefit of the discovery process is that it can be heavily social. You'll meet new, likeminded, motivated students, and you'll stretch your social bounds. You'll come into contact with great faculty who enjoy investing in you. You'll be exposed to resources and opportunities that you can't replace or duplicate in the classroom. You must participate in life in order to learn about yourself.

Some of the student activities and organizations you are considering might be an uncomfortable stretch for you. Do them anyway. As one very successful student said to me, "I was told to take the path of most resistance, and it paid off." You will be amazed at what you learn and the confidence you build by doing what you have the option not to do. Discovering what you don't like to do, what you are not naturally good at, is as important as discovering what you enjoy.

Another area that will help you in the discovery process is work experience. I would encourage you to try your hand at as many different work experiences as you can. Try working as a waiter, construction/laborer, lifeguard, cashier, knife salesperson, bank teller, retail salesman, caddie, tutor, or volunteer for a politician. The more the merrier.

Each of these work experiences will expose you to new situations, skill sets, likes, dislikes, and opportunities for growth. Take opportunities to test drive different talents or interests. It's only by putting yourself in scenarios like these that you will truly be in the discovery process and be able to evaluate what you enjoy and what draws you.

Speaking to an industrious student, I once asked what type of summer work she was currently engaged in. She said, "For the past three years, I have been working as a lifeguard at the town pool. It's a great job, pays well, and is pretty easy." Though I understand the attraction of coming back to that job a second and third year, my discovery question is: what was she learning in the second and third year that she did not learn in the first?

Variety not only serves you because it exposes you to different experiences and activities; it is also beneficial during the interview process. Working as a waiter for four years performing virtually the same tasks means that you have probably had a fairly narrow scope of experiences. When you have held a number of different positions, the interviewer can get a sense of how you work and excel in different environments, how you work for different personalities, and how well you learn and adopt new skill sets. Variety keeps you from being seen as one-dimensional. The other important benefit is that a variety of experiences opens up opportunities to find common ground and build a better rapport with the hiring manager.

When students begin to value experiences, stretching, learning, and growing, their perspective toward their studies and classes improves because they can begin to see how work and the classroom tie together. The question becomes not *How much can I earn?* but *How much can I learn?* How can I grow and stretch and to what new experiences can I be exposed? I understand that the desire for good, maybe even relatively easy money is strong. But your pursuit of your gifts and calling needs to be stronger if you want to be hired 'right' out of college.

The question becomes not *How much can I earn?* but *How much can I learn?*

When you are in the discovery process, your views of investing your time and maximizing your summer work experiences change. In some cases, it doesn't matter what you're doing, as long as you're doing something different and you're in the pursuit of discovering. Remember, you want to discover your talents as accurately and as soon as possible.

Getting Busy:

1. **Visit your Student Affairs office or go online and see what activities are available. Here are a few ideas:**
    - Join and serve in a fraternity or sorority
    - Compete on the debate team
    - Work as a teacher's assistant to a department or professor
    - Become a campus tour guide
    - Serve on the Homecoming Committee
    - Volunteer or work in career services
    - Play, manage, or coach intramural sports
    - Become a Resident Assistant
    - Serve in student government
    - Serve on the student judicial board
    - Participate in campus ministries
    - Become involved in an honor society
    - Write for the campus newspaper or radio
    - Participate in one of the many facets of a musical or drama
    - Become a big brother/sister or a mentor
    - Serve as a tutor
    - Join and actively participate in a charity
    - Consider ROTC or another military service[7]
        - These options offer a tremendous opportunity for experiences, training, and growth.

Once you have selected your activities, invest in them. Seek to understand what it takes to be successful in them. The difference between being a member and an active member is significant. You can simply be a name on a membership list of a fraternity or sorority, an active member serving and growing in the Greek system, or one of its members who serves an office such as President or Greek ambassador. Imagine what you could learn and be exposed to while engaged at those various levels!

---

[7] The military is a great option for those who are unsure about what they want to study or even if they should attend college. The military is a great place to gain exposure to different career options, it can help pay for college, and always looks amazing on a résumé.

2. **Before you pick an activity or two, decide what type of skills, talents, and experiences you would like to gain. Once you have those identified, picking the 'right' activity will be easier.**

3. **There may be some wisdom in sticking with one long-term activity for several years.**
    *   First, this shows future employers that you can stay committed to and focused on an activity.
    *   Second, you might consider staying with a particular activity if there appears to be opportunity to *continue to grow* and earn greater responsibility that would benefit your discovery.

<u>Note:</u> Look for activities that involve training. For example, working as a Resident Assistant, working at career services, or joining the debate team will expose you to workshops and training sessions that add to your skill sets.

Case Study
Vanessa Finds a Win/Win/Win

Vanessa bounces into career services bursting with excitement. "Morning, Dianne. I know I'm a bit early, but I wanted to gather my thoughts before I met with the big guy."

"Make yourself at home, dear."

Vanessa makes her way to the conference room, unpacks, and gets to work. She wants to tell Mr. Simms how she approached picking an activity. She feels really good about her methodology and her final decision.

"Hello, V."

"Oh. Hi there, Mr. Simms. I didn't even hear you."

"I need to apologize. I have only a few moments, meetings all day."

"Great, I'll cut to the chase. I went online to the school's website. I couldn't believe how many choices there were; it was pretty overwhelming. I narrowed it down to a dozen or so. Then I saw Mrs.

Bryan on Monday, and she helped me narrow my search down to three choices. She gave me the names of a few students who are participating in each activity, and I contacted and interviewed them."

"Interviewed them? Very interesting, go on."

"I wanted to see what they were getting out of each activity and how it would relate to me. Mr. Simms, I have a limited amount of time, and if I'm going to be busy—I'd like to be busy with a purpose."

"Excellent. So tell me what you found."

"I narrowed it down to three activities. Here is a short description of the skills I would be exposed to in each:"

1. <u>Campus Tour Guide</u>: public speaking, the need to organize, networking, planning, interpersonal communication, developing the art of conversation and small talk, memorizing facts and figures, selling and marketing, answering questions on the spot, leading small and large groups, working under pressure, developing the ability to adapt as weather impacts tours, encouraging school pride, working alone, being a spokesperson, and possibly handling contentious situations.

2. <u>Resident Assistant (RA)</u>: leadership, mentoring, counseling, crisis management, decision-making, being responsible, handling authority, leading group activities, upholding campus and dorm standards, role modeling, event planning, time management, scheduling, and conflict resolution.

3. <u>Debate Team</u>: critical thinking, teamwork, meeting deadlines, working under pressure, ad-libbing, leadership, analytical thinking, preparation, organization, memorizing facts and figures, extemporary arguing, public speaking, logic, reasoning, and following direction.

"Vanessa, this is impressive; you are really taking this seriously."

"The list for each is not exhaustive, but I was amazed by what each of these experiences can provide. It's like having a second education, and many of these skills I can't learn in the classroom."

"The suspense is killing me. Which one did you pick?"

"I didn't pick one."

"You didn't? After all this?"

"I picked two. I'm going to be a campus tour guide, and, get this, they need a replacement RA immediately because one just quit. I already applied and interviewed for the RA position. Mr. Simms, I was so afraid of letting these experiences go that I decided I'm going to participate in both."

"Both! Now that's impressive. I know you won't regret it. However, have you considered the impact on your grades?"

"I'll just need to be more efficient with my time. I reviewed the time assessment you had assigned me earlier and found that I do have lots of time, I just need to be more discerning in how I invest it. I was busy, really busy, but not with a purpose. Keeping my grades up and participating in these activities will be a challenge, but I think the investment in me is worth it. I'm actually excited. Do you want to hear the best part?"

"Of course. But first let me say that this is terrific. You've approached this just like an interview process. You've done your research, conducted informational interviews, and gone through the pros and cons of each activity. You're truly investing in the discovery process. So what's the best part?"

"What's unique about being a campus tour guide and an RA is that they both require a great deal of training—and they are both paid positions. I'm going to get all this training, experience, exposure, and they're going to pay me."

"Wow! Experience, training, and pay; that's a win-win-win situation. It's great to see you so excited. I remember that earlier this semester, a young woman who looked a lot like you came in confused and uncertain. Isn't it remarkable what happens when you become invested in the discovery process?" Mr. Simms leans forward and gives Vanessa an enthusiastic high-five.

"Look at that list, Vanessa. The skills you'll be developing are life skills that are valuable in every occupation. They are priceless. What makes these skills even more remarkable is that most of them are not found in a classroom but in activities and experiences. Exposing yourself to these types of activities will serve you in so many ways. Strengthening your E will be invaluable during your job interviews."

"Strengthening my E?"

"Yes, Vanessa. Remember the strength of your road map is the experiences you have had and the ones you will participate in. Your E is the most important piece of the discovery puzzle."

"Ah, E is for experience. The I is the inward call. I imagine O will be revealed later?"

"Yes, Vanessa, soon. Since you are so motivated, I guess now would be a good time for another assignment."

"What? Can't I just bask in my accomplishments for a few days?"

"Have I led you astray yet? It's time to interview."

"I'm not ready for that. I haven't picked my major yet. No way."

"No. A different kind of interview." Mr. Simms goes on to explain just what he means, hands Vanessa a list of questions, and rushes to his meeting.

CHAPTER 11

Listening for the Outward Call
Listen to Your Fans

"We are always more anxious to be distinguished for a talent which we do not possess, than to be praised for the fifteen which we do possess."

Mark Twain

There is something essential that we need to add to our evaluations and assessments of our own gifts, talents, likes, and dislikes. Remember our *American Idol* scenario where contestants were absolutely convinced that they had incredible voices, only to hear from the professionals that they in fact did not even have a mediocre voice? We need an additional piece to our puzzle: the outside voice.

We need others to balance our insights. There's a proverb that says, "Above all else, the heart is deceitful." We believe what we want to believe, and sometimes the view we have of ourselves is a bit...distorted.

Now that you have begun the hard work of listening to the inward call, you need to listen for the outward call. The great news is that like the inward call, the outward call has been occurring throughout your life.

Have you ever heard people say that someone is a natural? A natural what? An athlete, a singer, a writer, an orator, a debater, a teacher, an accountant, or a leader? What we mean when we say that someone is a natural is that he seems to perform a particular task or skill with ease and grace, as if he was born to do it. Let's be fair; these people were not just born this way. Michael Jordon, for one, wasn't born the best basketball player; he took raw, natural talent and built on it. The initial raw talent needs to be there in order to build the rest of the masterpiece. What we are trying to do is discover your raw and natural talents.

The outward call is listening to what others think you are good at, what others say your gifts, talents, and skills are. What do others recognize and see in you? The strength of the outward call depends on one's experiences. If you have not been busy with a purpose, then there will be few opportunities for others to observe your strengths, gifts, and aptitudes. If you have been busy, who should you ask? Consider parents, longtime and new friends, siblings, leaders at your place of worship, teachers, professors, coaches, family friends, bosses, classmates, and mentors. All these people know you in some capacity and have observed and evaluated you. What they see is important. Their opinions, combined with your thoughts, will help bring your career path into focus.

My favorite among this group would be your parents or guardians. Believe it or not, they actually know you well and can offer important insights—if you're humble and willing to listen. I've had many conversations over the years with parents who are worried and frustrated by the job market and their current graduate's struggles with finding a career. When I press them about what they think their son or daughter would be successful at, I am often amazed at their insights.

On a plane ride home, I met a man, Steve, who after hearing about what I do for a living, quickly expressed his concern about his daughter who had just moved back home because she could not find work. "She has interviewed with a dozen companies, and no one will hire her," he said with a sigh.

I inquired about her major and current job pursuits. He shared with me that she was a biology major and has been interviewing for lab positions. "I don't understand it. She's a good student and a terrific kid; she would be an asset to any company."

After thinking for a moment, I asked him, "When you and your wife close your eyes and imagine your daughter working, what do each of you see her doing? Is it lab work?"

He thought and then began to smile. "Funny you should ask that. We don't see her in the lab."

"Really? Where do you see her?"

"She has a dynamic personality and is amazing with people; we always pictured her in sales or out in front of a crowd, not in a quiet lab."

I share this story to illustrate that there are times we think we know ourselves, yet others have a different view of us. Maybe we are right, maybe those who know us best are correct, or maybe it's a combination of both. As you look for your gifts, you need to tap into others who may help you see them or at least provide a different point of view and perspective. By listening to the outward call and the inward call, you are going to get a better idea of where you should go next.

My assessment, which I relayed to this father on the plane, was that maybe the reason his daughter was unable to land a lab job was that the interviewers had seen her true gifts and talents and realized her strengths did not match the needs for the company's position. I suggested that perhaps the interviewers saw what the parents knew all along: her personality and experiences would not be a long-term fit in a lab position. I suggested that his daughter enter into the discovery process, find her gifts, and apply them in a more suitable profession.

These types of conversations can and should occur with those who have observed you over time and have interacted with you. These interviews can be with coaches, professors, best friends, and academic advisors who have watched you grow. There are literally dozens of people you could interview. Remember: Not everything they say is accurate, but take the information and consider it.

Not everything they (coaches, professors, best friends, and academic advisors) say is accurate, but take the information and consider it.

Those who know us well are excellent resources in our attempt to find our career path. The outward call adds that invaluable piece to the puzzle: outside input based on experiences, observation, and care from those that may have a vested interest in our development and success.

It's time to start interviewing—not for jobs, but for the input from friends, family, colleagues, and fellow students. Increase the volume of the outward call by engaging others and listening to what they see in you.

Time to Seek the Outward Call:

1. **Make a list of people you know, and circle five to ten who know you in different capacities.**
   - If possible, you want people such as parents, guardians, and close relatives who have known you for a long time. You also would like a few who have seen you in action: past bosses, supervisors, teachers, coaches, and colleagues. Round the list off with some friends, acquaintances, and fellow students.

2. **Prepare a sample letter. Here is an example:**

   I'm in the exciting process of figuring out what I'd like to study and pursue as a career. I've gathered many important pieces to this puzzle, but there is one left in which you can play a valuable role.

   I'm trying to get a better grasp of what I would like to do as a profession. I have many likes and interests. I want to seek input from people who I know are thoughtful and whom I respect. Would you mind speaking candidly about your experiences with me and what you have observed? Your answers will be added to other interviews I am conducting and will be helpful in this discovery process.

   Would you be willing to schedule an appointment to meet with me? I look forward to hearing from you.

3. **Meet with your prospects to gain insights through the interview process by asking:**
   (Be sure to lay the ground rules beforehand. Let your interviewees know that you are looking for honesty and candor.)

   - <u>Thinking about our interactions, what are some adjectives or nouns you might use to describe me?</u>
     - Look and listen for these types of answers: social/private, leader/follower, independent/dependent, introvert/extrovert, compliant/dominant, and dependable/ needs direction.

- Remember what was discussed in Chapter 5: Seek Feedback: be humble, listen, and solicit opportunities for growth.

- <u>Do you see any particular skills, talents, or gifts that I possess?</u>
  - Look and listen for these types of answers: good communicator or writer, good with details and analytics, natural organizer, a gift for hospitality, great with kids or groups, detail-oriented, a natural with numbers, science, money, people, animals, or writing.

- <u>What are the top two descriptors and noted skills?</u>

- <u>When you think of me, post-graduation in the working world, what do you see or picture me doing? Why?</u>

- <u>When thinking about a career for me, what advice would you give to me?</u>

- <u>Do I remind you of anyone with whom you've worked? What similarities do we share, and what is that individual doing today?</u>

Case Study
Here It Is: the Outward Call

Vanessa glances at the interview sheet and pages through it. *Interviews?* Turning the front sheet over, she begins to read through the questions and smiles. "I found the O," she says aloud as she makes her way toward the door.

"You found what?" Dianne asks.

"I found the O in the AEIOU formula. I'm supposed to interview people I know so that I can hear the..." Vanessa skims the first paragraph. "Here it is, the outward call."

"You're quick, Vanessa. Good luck, I hope you hear it loud and clear."

"Thanks, Dianne. I'll need it."

On the way home, Vanessa rereads the premise behind the interviews. She hurries to her room and begins compiling a list of possible interviewees. At the top of the list are her mom and dad. They are followed by her high school soccer coach, her boss at the restaurant, her theater coach, and her best friend.

I'll start with these questions and I'll add a few of my own. Vanessa opens her email account and begins the process of setting up her interviews.

CHAPTER 12

Intentional Involvement

Focus on Your Strengths

"Great ability develops and reveals itself increasingly with every new assignment."

Baltasar Gracian

In Chapter 4: Begin the Discovery Process, I discussed being busy with a purpose. I did so to encourage you to maximize the activities which would help you in your discovery process. As your discovery process begins to produce results, you will want to remain busy but to increase your focus on that which will help you grow and what will confirm what you believe are your areas of interests and strength. You are moving from *busy with a purpose* to *intentional involvement.*

Discovering your gifts and talents is only the start of your journey. You must begin to invest in them. You have begun to uncover and discover your gifts. Through experiences and listening to your inward and outward call, you have identified a list of gifts and talents that you think might be worth investing in. Investing means finding activities and experiences that help you hone and confirm which gifts, talents, and skill sets you would like to pursue.

Let me address the topic of ability. In your discovery process, you may have encountered an ability or talent and are wondering how that should fit into your decision to become intentionally involved. Being able to perform a skill or task doesn't necessarily qualify one for a profession or calling. For example, I may be *able* to be an accountant (e.g., know how to add and subtract numbers, balance my own checkbook), but that doesn't qualify as a natural ability or gifting. The difference is that my accountant friends enjoy their work; I wouldn't. They possess the natural skill, temperament, and talent for that profession. My gifts point elsewhere.

Being able to perform a skill or task doesn't necessarily qualify one for a profession or calling.

My good friend, Jim, is a professional singer. He has one of those voices that makes you smile because you can't believe how incredible it is. He has the foundational tools, the inward call, and the outward call; he's right where he belongs. He and others recognized his talent, and he became intentional in his activities. These activities and experiences began to maximize the discovery process, helping him confirm and hone his skills. He invested countless hours in studying and practicing his art. He loves performing because he has the gift for it.

Andy, another great friend, is an artist as well. His canvas is 2x4s, power tools, and dust. He creates and builds such amazing structures; fine woodworking is natural to him. He just envisions it and creates it. He recognized his talents early and confirmed them by being intentional in his pursuit of work and experiences. He too has invested many hours of practice in perfecting his skill, but again, he started with the raw talent.

I envy them both. I know that with lots of practice, I could be a better singer and woodworker, but I don't believe that I possess the aptitude, talents, drive, and temperament to succeed in either of those callings. While my friends have gifts that I don't have, I'm not frustrated, because I know that I have gifts, talents, and temperaments that others don't. We either have 'em or we don't. Everyone has a unique set of aptitudes.

Your full-time job at college is not only to be a student in class, but also a student of you.

Once you discover your gifts, and you possess the drive to succeed, you must engage in intentional activity in order to confirm and develop them. Each of the examples above demonstrated a person's awareness of his gifts and his investment in refining those gifts. Jim, the singer, spent five to six years learning three languages and traveling to New York City several times a week to study and sing. He loved the process. He invested in his gifts and wound up winning the Young Pavarotti award—not by accident but on purpose! Your full-time job at college is not only to be a student in class, but also a student of you. That means being busy with a purpose and then transitioning to intentional involvement. You need to look for activities, clubs, and jobs that will test, refine, and hone your raw and natural gifts. Hopefully you will find joy in developing your gifts, and you will begin to naturally seek out career tracks and concentrations of study that will make best use of them.

Hone Your Talents. Become Intentional:

1. **Aptitudes:**
   - Have you inventoried your skills, likes, dislikes, and aptitudes?
   - Have you completed and reviewed an aptitudes assessment?

2. **Experiences:**
   - Have you sought a variety of activities and experiences that will expose you to new scenarios and stretch you? In Chapter 4: Begin the Discovery Process, you were encouraged to be busy with a purpose. Have you begun?

3. **Inward Call:**
   - Have you completed and evaluated your list of activities from Chapter 8: Listening for the Inward Call? Critique the jobs and experiences and what you learned or discovered about yourself. What did you enjoy or not enjoy about each?

4. **Outward Call:**
   - Being busy with a purpose gives others a better opportunity to observe your gifts. If you want to hear a louder, more accurate call, you must increase the number of experiences so that you *may* be observed.
   - Have you completed your interviews from Chapter 11: Listening for the Outward Call?
   - Do you see consistencies between your inward and outward call?

5. **Intentional involvement:**
   - Now take what you've learned in Chapter 4: Beginning the Discovery Process and invest in those skills and talents that you discovered.
   - Visit the Student Affairs office again. This time, look through the available clubs, activities, and experiences

that will help hone and confirm what you have been discovering.

- For example: if you have discovered that you have a
talent for writing and speaking, you might want to
join the debate team or school newspaper in order to
enhance and confirm these talents.

6. **Breaks:**
- Don't think of summer, spring, and holiday breaks as
opportunities to sleep in and hang out. See them as
opportunities to confirm and enhance skills in which
you believe you might want to invest in.
- For example: thinking of becoming a doctor? Try to
shadow a doctor for a week, helping her whenever
possible—all for free. (Free to her, but the payoff for
you is incalculable!)
- Other opportunities might include volunteering in a
hospital, ambulance squad, ER, clinic, hospice, or a
home healthcare company.
- You are going to gain insights and be challenged in a
way you *never* could in the classroom or on a couch.
- Offer to do all these for free if you need to. It will be
the best investment you can make because the return
is 'a more focused and informed you.'
- Furthermore, these experiences go on the résumé and
into your interviews.

Case Study
Interviews Help Vanessa Hear the O

Vanessa ends the phone conversation with her high school
coach and smiles. *Great memories. I'm so thankful I had Mr. Faulkner
as a coach.* Having concluded the last of her interviews, she types her
final thoughts, presses Print, and watches as five single-lined sheets
follow each other onto the outfeed tray. She reaches over and begins
to read through each interview, smiling several times. *Funny how people see me.*

The next morning, Vanessa brings Dianne a fresh cup of hazelnut coffee—light and sweet, of course.

"Well, hi there, Vanessa. Aren't you thoughtful. It smells heavenly. Why so chipper?"

"I'm excited. Two weeks ago when Mr. Simms and I met, he suggested I interview people. The interview process turned out to be really interesting."

"I'm glad. So you've figured it all out?"

"Not exactly, but I think I'm a lot further along."

"What's all the commotion out here?" asks Mr. Simms as he enters the room.

"Looks like your jumper has jumped," Dianne says with a smile.

"That's what I like to hear. Where did you land?"

"Mr. Simms, I finished interviewing, and it was great. I doubted you, but you were right!"

"Don't doubt me, V," Mr. Simms says through a big Cheshire Cat smile.

"Vanessa, the last thing he needs to hear is that he's right." Dianne rolls her eyes.

"Let's grab a seat in the conference room; tell me what you've discovered."

"Mr. Simms, I must say I was a bit skeptical and nervous. I didn't really want to bother anyone with this interview process, but each person I asked was willing. Each interview was pretty different and a lot of fun. Each recounted stories about me and gave fresh insights. It's amazing that people have so many vivid memories of me. It was very helpful."

"Did you see or recognize any patterns?"

"Not at first. But after my third or fourth interview, I began to hear similar phrases come up."

"Go on."

"For instance…" Vanessa opens up her binder, flips through the pages, and lands on a page full of highlights. "My first interview was with my boss from the restaurant where I worked the summer after my senior year in high school and my freshman year of college. She described me as 'outgoing' and a 'people person,' and said I 'did a great job of upselling.'" Vanessa explains to Mr. Simms that upselling is having people add desserts, coffee, or carryout items to their bill.

"My boss also remembers me as an outstanding mentor to new waitresses and waiters."

"Sounds pretty good so far. Do you agree with the comments?"

"Yes, I just wouldn't have picked out those qualities and memories. Wait until you hear this." Vanessa turns over two more pages and points. "This is my youth group leader at church. She said I was outgoing too." She looks up at Mr. Simms. "That descriptor appears five times in my interviews." She looks down at her notes again. "A team player, a great coach, and a motivator." She pauses, smiling.

"When I asked my soccer coach what he saw me doing, he said coaching a team someday. I already coach a youth team in my town during the summer."

"That sounds exciting. Seems there are some threads running through your interviews. Did you hear it?"

"Hear it?"

"Yes, Vanessa, the outward call. It's that voice we hear in others as they recognize our gifts and strengths. Listen for the moment when your inward call and your outward call meet."

"Yes, that occurred to me. Especially when I finished my interviews and began seeing patterns. Oh, by the way, I think I found the O in your AEIOU riddle. Cute."

Mr. Simms smiles. "AEIOU. A simple but powerful formula for success. Aptitudes are best discovered and expressed in a variety of experiences. Experiences help us hear and confirm the inward and outward call. Without experiences we are running blind. The more quality experiences..."

"The louder the call," Vanessa says triumphantly.

"It's time to fill in another segment of our Discovery Road Map. You can now see how AEI and O are coming together."

Vanessa looks at the diagram Mr. Simms has placed in front of her. "That makes perfect sense."

"Vanessa, do you like music?"

"I love music. Why do you ask?"

"Vanessa, if I gave you earphones that had one song playing into your left ear and a different song playing into your right ear, how would that sound?"

"Horrible. I think the word *torture* comes to mind."

"Why?"

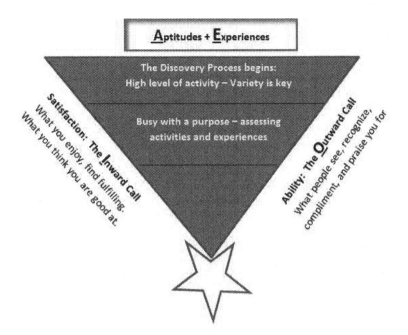

"Because the different beats, cadences, keys, and styles would clash with each other."

"Vanessa, we might say that the music lacked harmony. The word *harmony* originates from the Greek word 'harmonia,' which means: agreement, concord. The same principle applies to the inward and outward call: there needs to be harmony between the two."

"I love that analogy. I understand what you are saying. I feel that there is harmony in what I and others are seeing as my aptitudes."

"So tell me more about your interviews and the harmony you heard."

"I met with my parents for coffee over the weekend. They provided me with some good insights. My mom saw me on stage performing, and my dad saw me in sales of some sort. They also repeated several of the observations others had."

"So what are your conclusions?"

"No conclusions yet. I'm going to finish this semester in my undeclared major, but I'm going to pursue three specific activities. First, I absolutely love being a campus tour guide; second, I'm loving my RA experience, which I hope to continue next year; and third, I'm going to audit a public speaking course being held on Tuesday and Thursday nights."

"This is all well and good, but how does this focus you on your goals?"

"I was very interested by a conversation I had with the dad of one of my friends. He's not someone I officially interviewed, but these days I find myself interviewing anyone who sits with me. Anyway, he's a big wig in a company back in my hometown. He's in the training and development department of his company."

"I'm guessing you're leaning toward something like communications as a major."

"I thought about that, but I think instead I'm leaning toward business. Because I already have strong communication skills, I can find experiences and activities that will continue to enhance those. I feel drawn to a business major and maybe a minor in communications. Every company and industry has a training and development department, so I think a general business degree will be very helpful. Do you think that is the right major for me?"

"Vanessa, I'm thrilled for you and agree with your logic. You've done a great job with all these assignments. You've really embraced the discovery process and have some terrific information with which to make better choices."

"Thanks, Mr. Simms, but do you think I'm picking the right major?"

"Vanessa, this may surprise you. I don't believe there is always a 'right' major. Often gifts can be used and expressed in several different majors or career paths. For example, if your aptitudes lead you toward engineering, you could enroll in one of the many engineering majors here on campus. Your gifts could be used in one of many fields. You've made the right choice for you."

Often gifts can be used and expressed in several different majors or career paths.

"Thanks, Mr. Simms. I still have to work out a few issues, but I have you to thank."

"The difference between a decision you would have made on a major several months ago and the decision you make now is that this decision is based powerfully on AEIOU. Your experiences have produced the necessary evidence to make an informed choice."

"OK, I'll have to admit that when I first heard the AEIOU formula, I didn't think it would work, but I'm glad I stuck with it."

"Sometimes genius takes time to appreciate," Mr. Simms says. "On a more serious note, you have this great contact that is in the training and development department at a large corporation. Did you ever broach the subject of an internship?"

"I did, but he told me they actually cut back two positions in their department due to budget constraints."

"Vanessa, what happens if you work for free? They obviously need the help since now they are short-staffed."

"For free, all summer? I really need the money, Mr. Simms."

"Vanessa, this could be the best opportunity yet. Many times, internships are in reality a two to three month interview."

"Interview?"

Your experiences have produced the necessary evidence to make an informed choice.

"Yes. There you are working all summer long, hopefully displaying your work ethic, humility, integrity, and maturity all under the watchful eye of your supervisor. If you do a great job, which I know you will, they just might ask you back next summer. Either for pay or for free, but either way, you're buying experiences which are growing you as a professional and as a person. Take a look at the diagram. This is what your discovery process has looked like."

Vanessa points to the Discovery Road Map. "It's really quite simple. I started by having a broad range of experiences. Then as I continue to move down towards the point, my experiences become more and more focused as I discover and invest in particular gifts and talents."

"Now you can see that seeking an internship, even one without pay, can be a critical piece as you move towards being hired right. Let's fill in one more section: intentional involvement."

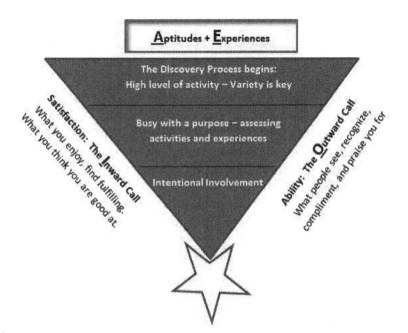

"I see. This internship will be an example of intentional involvement for me. I'll give him a call this evening and see what he thinks."

Vanessa looks at the time on her smartphone and jumps up. "Oh! I've a tour in twenty minutes. I need to go."

Mr. Simms and Vanessa walk toward the front door.

"I'm really proud of you, Vanessa. It sounds like you did the hard work of hearing the outward call, and it appears to agree with your inward call."

"Mr. Simms, that's the funny part. I knew I enjoyed teaching and performing, but it was only when these talents were confirmed by others that they really stood out to me. I gotta run, but I'll be back later this week."

With that, Vanessa pushes open the door and races off.

Mr. Simms spins around and looks at Dianne, who is waiting expectantly. He raises his arms and starts dancing around like a triumphant prizefighter.

"For Pete's sake, Mr. Simms, you're scaring the other students."

Mr. Simms looks around. "Who's next?"

CHAPTER 13

Grades Matter

Make Each Semester Count... Because It Will

"Give me six hours to chop down a tree, and I will spend the first four sharpening the axe."

Abraham Lincoln

All this talk about experiences, activities, and living certainly sounds fun and exciting, but you must realize that another part of the discovery process is your grades. Grades are important. They are a reflection of your ability to learn, comprehend, and apply knowledge. They are also an indicator of your ability to put your mind to a long-term task and accomplish it. Consistent good grades may also reflect a strong work ethic. You need to spend quality time and effort with your studies. Your grades may be a reflection of where your interests lie. That is why, as a recruiter, I spend time looking over transcripts.

I spent over ten years recruiting and hiring. I've had countless conversations with fellow managers regarding criteria they are looking for in new hires. When it comes to grades, rightly or wrongly, many managers have a GPA cutoff; for many, it is at least a 3.0. For those particular managers, if you don't have a 3.0, they are not going to interview you. In my book, *Hire on a WHIM,* I discuss the flaws of that philosophy. But today you should assume that hiring managers have a similar cutoff, so strive for good grades.

Here's the difficult news: if you have one rotten semester, you will have to string many good semesters to pull up that GPA. For example, if you bomb your first semester with a GPA of 2.1, as I did, you'll have to string seven, yes, *seven* straight semesters of a 3.1 or better to pull your overall GPA up over a 3.0. Do your best to avoid the one bad semester.

You might find yourself in a position where you've had several difficult semesters; don't panic. Recruiters will look at transcripts if you provide them. This gives you an opportunity to show your remarkable turnaround and strong finish. I love to see students, who after a bad semester or year, learned their lesson (no pun intended), changed their habits and study skills, and ended their years with a bang. It doesn't matter which scenario you find yourself in; grades are important! Though experiences provide the greatest opportunity for self-discovery, your performance in class matters. Make the grades!

Though experiences provide the greatest opportunity for self-discovery, your performance in class matters. Make the grades!

For recruiters, past behavior is the best predictor of future results. For example, if you have been a successful waitress in the past, I have every reason to believe you will be a successful waitress in the future. When it comes to grades, if you don't excel at learning in the college setting, there may be good reason to doubt that you can excel at learning in the working world.

There are certain majors where grades are essential. For example, majors such as accounting, pre-med, pre-law, and engineering are particularly purposeful and focused in their coursework. These majors specifically prepare students for a career in those particular fields. Grades in these majors reflect one's competency in these important foundational classes.

The combination of good grades and strong experiences are valuable when you begin interviewing for your first postgraduate position. This powerful combination is what you'll need in order to stand out from among your peers. In Chapter 4: Begin the Discovery Process, we saw that organizations often see recent graduates as risky hires because many are engaged in the discovery process *after* graduation, resulting in a higher turnover.

Keep in mind, each time a hiring manager interviews a candidate, his or her challenge is to find the right person for the position. Managers are looking for clues and concrete evidence that the candidate they are going to hire has the essentials to succeed. Those who have been actively engaged in the discovery process will be able to speak confidently about their skills, talents, and drive. Those candidates involved in the discovery process will also be able to point to very specific experiences, classwork, and life lessons which support why they are the 'right' candidate for the position. Whether they cognitively know it or not, hiring managers are looking, or should I say listening, for the harmony that should exist in your studies, classroom, and work experiences as well as the harmony between your inward and outward call. The combination of good grades and strong experiences is a powerful and valuable combination to both the hiring manager and to the candidate!

Grades Matter: Set the Academic Bar High:

1. **Evaluate your grades.**
   - What is your current GPA?
   - Are you satisfied with it?
   - What GPA would you like to have upon graduation?
   - What will it take for you to achieve it?
   - Do the math and plot your course.

2. **Making the grades begins with good planning.**
   - If you are going to implement my suggestions, you already realize that people who want to be hired 'right' out of college are going to be busy. So you must plan your days.
   - What is your plan?
   - Do you have a planning tool? Outlook™, a Day Timer™, or a web-based scheduler?
   - You must plan your work and then work your plan.

3. **If you have not done so yet, take a course in time management; most universities offer them.**

Note: I was able to graduate with a 3.1 even though I was extremely busy because I adhered to two philosophies:

   - My first philosophy was to never miss a class. Professors often use class to cover what they will eventually ask on a quiz or exam. I also knew that no one could take better notes for me than I could take for myself and that there was value in not just reading something but also hearing it. By the end of my four years, I missed only one class.
   - The second philosophy was to get a good night's sleep before an exam. Being sharp and well-rested was more valuable than last-minute cramming and an exhausted mind.

Understand how you learn, and put yourself in the best position for success.

Case Study
A Gift to Any Employer

Vanessa walks into the career services office and is met by Mr. Simms' assistant. "Hi, Allison. Is Mr. Simms in?"

"No, Mr. Simms had to head to lacrosse practice after work today. Team photos, you know. Anything I can help you with?"

Allison is a sharp young woman who graduated from Susque State just a few years ago. She stands just over six feet tall and has the look and charm of someone who was just transplanted from Charleston, S.C.

"All depends. Do you have a few minutes?"

"Sure, let's grab a seat."

Vanessa follows Allison and pulls out her transcripts. "I'm a little nervous about my grades. I mean, not these necessarily, they're pretty good but—"

Allison turns the sheet 180 degrees. "They look great to me." She flips to the second page. "These look great: GPA of 3.2. What's your concern?"

"I'd like to maintain my GPA, but I'm worried that I'm taking on too many extracurricular activities. Next year, I'll begin to take some of my focused coursework, and I imagine those classes will be more difficult and will require more time." Vanessa bites on the end of her pen and looks up at Allison with a nervous expression. "I'm taking on a lot of extra activities, which means I'm going to have *less* time to maintain grades in more difficult classes."

Allison quietly looks at the transcript. "Vanessa, I'll never talk anyone out of wanting to get better grades, but I think it's crucial to keep what's important in focus. Our philosophy here at career services is to help you find your talents and skills so that you are ready to be hired 'right' out of college. What you call *extra* activities we would consider *essential* activities. These activities bring tremendous value to who you are, to your overall education, and to the discovery process."

Vanessa sighs. "How do I balance it all and still make my grades?"

Allison smiles. "There are two issues here: time and your concern about the work being difficult. Let me address time first. Life is a series of opportunity costs, correct?"

"Econ 101; I remember it well. If you choose to do one thing, you do so at the expense of another."

"Exactly. Naturally, if you choose to invest in yourself and the discovery process, you will have less time for other activities, and that might have an effect on your grades. *Might.* But proper time management skills will help you find and create space in your days. The key is planning. Planning and using your time effectively will help you maintain the important balance between the discovery process, academics, and your social life. Balancing and planning will take work, but the effort will pay great dividends."

Vanessa sighs again. "I don't know. I'm just concerned. What about my job interviews and trying to explain away any drop in my grades? Are you going to be there to explain to the recruiter that I was trying to be busy with a purpose?"

Allison laughs. "I won't need to explain it—your résumé will. Your attitude, confidence, and experiences will. Vanessa, grades demonstrate one's ability to learn. But you bring a greater gift to the interview: an understanding of what you want to do with your career and why. You've done the extremely hard work of discovery, and that's a gift to any employer."

"Why is it a gift to them?"

Allison sits forward, and becomes animated. "Vanessa, according to a Leadership IQ study[8], 46 percent of newly-hired employees fail. Many times, it is not because of a lack of skill, but because of a poor fit. Those numbers are scary to employers because if they hire incorrectly, it is costly to the company, the hiring manager, and even to the new hire."

"Forty-six percent; that *is* scary."

"Being busy with a purpose and then being intentionally involved helps you beat those statistics. What a hiring manager sees and hears from someone who has been intentionally busy is evidence."

"Evidence?"

"Yes, evidence. Evidence that you have done the hard work of discovery and that your discovery has led you to that particular interview. Your work and classroom experiences on your résumé provide

---

[8] Why Employees Fail. Source: Leadership IQ. www.leadershipiq.com

the evidence a recruiter needs in order to make a confident hiring decision. She knows that you're more likely to fit in because the conclusion you have come to at the end of your four years of discovery has helped you decide that the position for which you are interviewing would be a good fit for you and your aptitudes. Plus, you have the experiences to back up your conclusions."

"Mr. Simms spoke about the discovery process being a legal term. If I continued with his analogy, my experiences are the evidence that I'm pointing to as I make my case to the employer as to why I'm the one for the position. The more time I invest in the discovery process—the stronger the evidence—the better my case will be to my prospective employer." Vanessa smiles as it all comes together. "I get it."

"Perfect. The second concern I heard you express is that the course load is going to be difficult. One of the great benefits of studying what we love and are designed to do is that it becomes relevant and exciting. Classes are no longer abstract, but applicable. We become internally motivated because we see the bigger picture. Students who become invested in the process, though they are busier than they have ever been, actually excel in their studies because they find a greater joy and purpose than before. Does that make sense?"

Vanessa smiles, nodding her head. "It does. It does."

CHAPTER 14

Sharpen Your Focus
The Picture Becomes Clearer

*"Always remember what you are good at
and stick with it."*
Ermenegildo Zegna

It's time to focus. By now, you should have filled out the Discovery Worksheet and finished your interviews. Are you listening to the inward and outward call? If so, you are well on your way to being more focused. As you develop and refine your list of skills, talents, likes, and aptitudes, you'll want to put them to the test. Visit the Student Affairs office again and see if there are activities that might provide even greater opportunity to focus. When you become intentionally busy, you will be actively pursuing your calling.

Experiences of all types are now opportunities to test and hone your gifts. Make each experience a learning lab, and truly test your assumptions. Were you correct? Were those you interviewed correct in their assessments of your gifts? Are you finding joy and satisfaction in these experiences? Are others recognizing your gifts? Continue to pursue these with a passion, and take every opportunity to explore them. Remember, it is through experiences that aptitudes are most effectively exposed and challenged.

Hopefully the discovery process has paid off and you are now in possession of the necessary evidence with which to build your case. What now? At this point, it may be obvious as to which direction you should go. If you have uncovered a great deal of evidence in this discovery process but are still struggling as to which major, field, or direction in which to invest, it may be time to seek additional counsel. Sit down with your parents or several people in the marketplace and have them review your conclusions. It's amazing what a few insightful questions can trigger.

The next step is to review the information with a counselor from the career services office at your university. These professionals are trained to help you transition from your classroom to your career. They can recommend great books. They can also offer you additional skill assessments which can help confirm and add valuable information to your decision-making process.

Other valuable resources are professors and faculty advisors. I'm a big fan of spending quality time with these people. They certainly can be a great source of information and advice. One word of caution: some of the faculty advisors are appointed as advisors because it is part of their job description. In other words, some faculty advisors are not appointed because they enjoy working with students or show a particular gift in providing wise counsel. You must be savvy and know that being an academic advisor by title does not automatically make one well-equipped for the position. Spend time getting to know your advisors so you can make that assessment. Are they generally interested in you and other students, and are they good listeners? Are they passionate about being an advisor? Do they have a good, strong reputation among your classmates and alumni? What do other professors think of them as advisors? There are some professors who have been teaching so long that even though they are experts in their subject matter, they may have lost a degree of relevance in today's marketplace. My point is: make sure you know whom you're speaking with and his *current* expertise in your field of interest.

I mentioned assessments you can take to help you identify your likes and dislikes. While these exercises can provide valuable insights, they may have some limitations. I spoke to a young professional who took a certain assessment three years in a row and received different results. Though her results were not dramatically different, there were variations. Remember, these assessments are to be part of the overall picture. Most of these tests have been validated, but I'd never recommend that these assessments be the sole source of your input when making academic or career decisions.

As you consider focusing, how are you going to invest your time during winter and summer breaks? Now is the time to try to find positions that will expose you to some of the career opportunities that may lie in your field of study. Depending on the strength of the economy and where you live, the amount and the quality of opportunities are going to vary. But one thing is usually consistent: companies are looking for excellent help. Your career services department may be able to help you find internships. Start there. If you cannot find an internship that pays, take one without pay. Though you are working without pay, you are not working for free. You are actually being paid in experience and exposure. The experiences can all be placed on a résumé, and few recruiters are going to ask or care if you were paid. Recruiters will, however, be impressed that you have acquired relevant and practical experience.

If you cannot find an internship that pays, take one without pay.

Internships have the potential to be one of the most valuable learning opportunities available to those in the discovery process. If you choose to invest in the internship process, you will find a great environment in which to grow. One of the results that occurs after working in a professional environment is that you begin to see yourself in a different light. You see and feel the connection between your classes and a potential career. Studies, projects, papers, and case studies now come alive like never before. It is akin to walking through a model home at a construction site and then walking through your home currently under construction. All the mess, noise, dust, garbage, and chaos make sense; it is all part of the process of building your home. It is worth it because you have seen and experienced the final product.

Take every opportunity to seek out work, either paid or unpaid, to further your exposure and insights into possible career tracks. You will deepen your understanding of the types of skills and talents needed to compete and succeed. You will also see how much more relevant your studies will be. You may discover through these experiences that there are certain aspects of the target job market that don't appeal to you. Knowing what you don't like is as valuable as learning what you do like because it helps you make important decisions based on facts and experiences, not on hopes and misunderstood dreams.

Focus = Intentional Involvement:

1. **In School:**
   - Review your list of skills, talents, and gifts.
   - Challenge each of them and make sure there is evidence of an inward and outward call for each.
   - Spend time with people who know you well. Discuss your list and possible majors or fields of study.
   - Make an appointment with career services and your professors and have a similar discussion about your gifts and possible majors or fields of study.
   - If you have narrowed your areas of interest down to a few choices, interview faculty and several alumni who have graduated in those majors. Determine whether the desired career track and your goals complement your gifting.

2. **Out of School:**
   - Look for experiences which will augment your understanding of the job market and marketplace.
   - Whether you are being paid or not, seek opportunities that will provide relevant experiences and exposure. The payoff will be significant.
   - At the end of each experience, evaluate what you liked and disliked. Do you visualize yourself working in that field and in that type of environment?
   - Can you project yourself into that company, that position? At this point, visualization can become a great motivator. For example, seeing yourself as a professional excelling in the Acme Company will be a powerful internal motivator during your remaining semesters at college.
   - Have you begun to network? More on networking in Chapter 16: Don't Jump without a Net, but networking needs to begin now.

Case Study
Investing in Her Summer

"Hello there, stranger. Where have you been?" Dianne asks cheerfully.

"With finals and all, I've just been swamped. How are things here?"

"Great. This is such a great time of the year for us: students interviewing, receiving job offers, leads, and internships. It's such a treat to see it all coming together."

"Is Mr. Simms in?"

"He's in there, dear." Dianne motions to the conference room.

Vanessa leans into the room. "Knock, knock."

"Hey, V. How did finals go? Come on in; have a seat."

"They went really well. Hey, congrats on your lacrosse team. I hear you're off to the Eastern Regionals later this week."

"I've got a terrific bunch of young men. Hard-working with great attitudes. Our goal now is to get to Nationals. I think we can do it."

"I'm sure you will, Mr. Simms. Before I leave for the summer, I want to say thanks for all your help this year. I don't think I'd be as focused as I am right now without your team's help."

"V, you did all the work. Just like my boys heading to Regionals. They've done the hard work in practice, in studying the films, in working on the basics, and here they are. I can only coach; I've got to have the willing audience in order to look good."

"True. I start my free internship two days after I get back home."

"You're going to love it. Tell me, what are you doing?"

"How can you say I'm going to love it if you don't even know what I'm doing?" Vanessa laughs.

"Vanessa, as you know, you're moving from busy with a purpose to intentional involvement." Mr. Simms pulls out the completed Discovery Road Map and slides it over.

"So this is where I am going." Vanessa points to the bottom star. "And the easiest way to get there is to focus on my strengths, be intentionally involved, and listen to the I and the O."

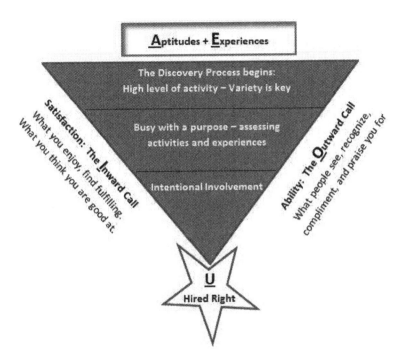

"Which leads to U being hired 'right.'"

"Nice. I'm looking forward to that day, but first I need to get the most out of this internship."

"That's it, Vanessa. Great internships don't just happen: they are nurtured. An internship is a two way street. Be mindful that your goals and the company's goals may be different. Do you know what you want out of this internship? If so, write your goals down and do your best to achieve them. I know you'll be in the discovery process all summer long. I feel sorry for the people you are reporting to. They are going to be peppered with questions every day. "

"You bet I'll be asking questions. Thanks for the reminder about writing down my goals. I'll definitely do that and share them with my manager. Hopefully our goals are similar and if not, at least I'll know up front. It's going to be a great opportunity; I plan on learning everything I can. I'm working at my friend's dad's company. Unfortunately, he didn't have a position for me in training, so I'll be starting in the accounting department. Not my first choice, but it's a good company and I figure eventually everything and everybody comes through accounting. So it will be an opportunity to gain exposure to different people in the company."

"I like your strategy." Mr. Simms glances at the time. "I'm preparing a student for an interview now; I've got to run. If you need anything over the summer, you know where to find me."

Vanessa stands up with Mr. Simms and gives him a warm hug. "Thanks for everything. Good luck at Regionals; know that I'll be cheering for you."

"My pleasure, V. Have a great summer; I'll see you in the fall. Call me if you need me."

CHAPTER 15

AEIOU into Action

Gain Some Exposure

"He who is outside the door has already a good part of his journey behind him."

Dutch proverb

It's time to jump into the marketplace. You are actively involved in experiences that are honing or challenging the skills, talents, and gifts that have been revealed in the discovery process. I want you to begin thinking about the summer. Yes, even if it is still September. Consider how you are going to continue the confirmation process. Regardless of pay, you need to find work experiences that will expose you twice.

Internships are one of the most valuable experiences in the discovery process. What is an internship? If you look at some of the synonyms of internship, you will find words like practicum, fellowship, residency, position, and training program. They all hit the heart of what an internship is: it's a time of testing and evaluation. Don't get nervous or stressed about the need to apply for an official internship. In my book (literally), an internship is defined as any experience, paid or unpaid, that exposes you to an industry or skill set to help you in your discovery process.

Look for experiences that will expose you twice. First, look for experiences that expose you to the type of work or career track for which you believe you are most suited. Don't get hung up on finding work doing exactly what you eventually want to do. Find an experience that will get you closer to where you want to end up than where you are now. For example, if you believe your gifts, talents, and calling point toward sales and that you have an interest in pharmaceutical sales, I'd encourage you to get involved in experiences that relate to that industry. Perhaps you could work in a doctor's office, a retail pharmacy, or in a hospital. All these expose you to healthcare and medicine, broadening your understanding of the field and market-place. If you can find a job in the pharmaceutical industry, take it, even if it is unrelated to sales. Another option is to take *any* sales posi-tion, regardless of its relevance to pharmaceuticals. Thus, you can be exposed to the skills and life of a sales professional.

Find an experience that will get you closer to where you want to end up than you are now.

Why work in the accounting department of a pharmaceutical company when you want to work in sales? One reason is that when you are inside the industry you learn a great deal about how it oper-ates, the culture, whether the industry is contracting or expanding. Another is you will meet colleagues who have come from other com-panies inside and outside your desired industry. They can share their thoughts, insights, experiences, and the pros and cons of companies and industries.

These positions help you see the arena that you are headed for and also allow you to begin to test your gifts. Even if the position you take is not directly related to where you would like to end up, it will expose you to elements and nuances that will be valuable in your deci-sion-making process.

The second way in which you will be exposed is to employ the networking advice in the next chapter: these experiences expose you to individuals and scenarios that may help in the near future. Even though you are looking for pharmaceutical sales, taking a summer job in the accounting department of a pharmaceutical company is going to expose you to employees who might be able to connect you to the right people or departments. While on the inside, you have opportu-nities to conduct informational interviews and meet other profes-sionals for coffee or lunch. They may be able to shine new insights into the desired position and career track. All these experiences give evidence of your efforts to invest in yourself. When interviewing you years from now, a prospective employer will appreciate your efforts to gain valuable, relevant experience for the job for which you are currently interviewing. These efforts speak volumes to the reality that you know what you want to do. That is extremely comforting to a prospective employer.

Work experiences are all valuable additions to a résumé. Each of these jobs is infinitely more valuable than run-of-the mill summer work. At the end of the summer, you will probably have the opportunity to have an official review of your work with those to whom you have reported. These reviews will also provide valuable opportunity for a professional to review your skills, gifts, and talents. These individuals can be a resource as you continue in the discovery process, and they may be willing to write a recommendation.

A well-executed internship is the culmination of the AEIOU formula for success.

You may not realize it, but by the end of the summer you will have completed a two to three-month-long interview. This experience might open opportunities for additional work on short school breaks or even provide a launching pad for course projects. If you've done an excellent job, you might be asked back to complete another internship, perhaps turning an unpaid internship into a paid one. If you apply next summer to this company or industry, you will have an internal recommendation. The knowledge you gain from this experience will be invaluable as you proceed in your career as a student and as a professional.

A well-executed internship is the culmination of the AEIOU formula for success. Understanding and discovering your aptitudes through a wide variety of experiences is the first step in identifying what you enjoy and are good at. You then begin to test the call by being busy with a purpose and then continue the confirmation by becoming intentionally involved. Hopefully by the end of the summer, your aptitudes will be in harmony with these calls and in the aptitudes they reflect! Movement through this process should be harmonious. If for some reason a discord is struck, stop and evaluate where this dissonance has occurred. The result of moving through this process will have you headed in the direction your calling lies.

The Search for Relevant Work Experience:

1. **What are you doing now to begin your search for an internship?**
   - Don't think just summer work; you have a long holiday break as well.
     - Spending any time in industry will be valuable.
     - Long breaks are great opportunities to shadow someone. Shadowing someone is simply spending a day or two following them around in order to get a better perspective of a particular career choice.
   - Visit career services for a list of companies that have provided internships in the past.
   - Contact your professors and academic advisors for names and contacts.
   - Speak with those whom you know in the industry or field.
   - Do not wait. Work on setting up an internship now.

2. **Be open to working an unpaid internship.**
   - If you do the hard work of networking, developing relationships with coworkers, and investing in the position, the benefits will outweigh the lack of pay.
   - Considering an unpaid position will also open more opportunities for you.
   - Having a talented, young professional work for free should be an easy package to sell to an employer, especially if budgets are tight.

3. **During an internship:**
   - Be an active student/employee by asking questions.
   - Set goals and objectives. Complete as many as possible.
   - Network inside and outside the department.
   - Seek feedback. Be open, humble, and ready to learn.
   - Ask more questions and present your business card.
   - Look for stretching opportunities.
   - Work hard and exceed expectations.
   - Spend time evaluating your gifts.
   - Ask even more questions.

4. **At the end of the internship:**
   - Seek to have an official review.
     - The review process can prove helpful.
     - The written evaluation could be worth its weight in gold.
   - Be humble when hearing opportunities to improve. Remember: You have professionals evaluating your work; their insights about you could play an important role in your discovery (a possible *American Idol* moment).
   - Seek another opportunity with the same company during the next break or summer vacation.
     - Try to diversify. Can you serve in the same department but in a different capacity?
     - Can you serve in another department?
     - Do they have opportunities in different locations?

5. **The end of the internship is the beginning of a relationship:**
   - Keep in touch with those you worked with:
     - Reach out periodically to ask questions, make inquiries, or even just to say, "How are you doing?"
     - Seek their professional advice. This can help deepen relationships since they are investing in you.
     - Let them know what and how you are doing (grades, classes, activities).
     - What can you do for them?
     - Ask if you can use them as a reference.

6. **Not all internships are created equal:**
   - Do you know what you are looking for in an internship?
     - Are there certain skill sets you are hoping to develop?
     - Are you looking for exposure to a particular work environment or business process?
     - Are you looking to develop relationships in a particular company or industry?
     - Contact a former intern and perform an informational interview. Determine what their goals were and if they were met.

- What did the former interns like and dislike about their experience?
- Know the company's goals, objectives, and agenda of the internship you are applying for.

7. **Explore job shadowing:**
   - Spend a day or two following, watching, and casually interviewing someone who is working in the industry in which you are interested.
   - Shadowing combined with an informational interview will significantly increase your understanding of your pending career path.
   - Shadowing and informational interviews should never be a clandestine attempt at seeking a job or interview. Be upfront and transparent when requesting to shadow or interview someone. Let the person know your intentions.

8. **Explore careers virtually:**
   - Visit CandidCareer.com to watch and listen to thousands of real candid informational video interviews with professionals from all industries. Watch as they speak about their careers, likes, dislikes, challenges, rewards, and share advice. See and hear what it takes to be successful in various callings. The small fee may be money well spent.

Case Study
The Internship Pays Off

"Hi, Vanessa; welcome back. Mr. Simms and I were just talking about you."

"It's good to be back; I had a great summer. RA orientation has been awesome, and I'm really learning a lot."

"There's our newest professional," Mr. Simms says, rounding the corner.

"Hi, Mr. Simms; it's good to see you."

"Reading your tweets and the emails you sent me, I got the sense that you were enjoying your internship. Tell me about your time."

"Mr. Simms, Susque Corp. is a great company—not what I expected. I've driven by the gated campus since I was a kid, and it always seemed stark and cold. I was wrong; the people were warm, inviting, and very helpful. I felt like I was part of the Susque family."

"What did you learn?"

"I learned that I never want to work in collections."

"Those must have been a long three months," Mr. Simms says.

"No. That's what was so great about this internship; it was broken up into three three-week segments. Each segment I worked in a different department."

"Excellent. Which was your favorite?"

"Collections was my least favorite. I don't think I was very good at it either. But I still worked hard. I tried to learn everything I could from that experience."

"It must've made for some long days," Dianne says in a comforting tone.

"There were some long days, but I learned a lot about myself and what I don't like. It's funny. During the first few days they had me observe the collections center. These professionals made it look so easy that I thought it would be a cinch. Boy, was I wrong."

"You know, I hear the same thing," Mr. Simms says, leaning against Dianne's desk. "People say that I make this job look so easy. Everyone thinks they can do it, and then they try it and realize that it takes a skill that…"

Dianne raises her hand and signals him to stop.

"Continue, dear," she says.

"What? It does take skill," Mr. Simms protests.

"Anyway, I learned the job was a lot harder than these professionals made it look. Guys, I realized that the position ultimately did not line up with my inward and outward calling. I know for sure that collections is not for me. Even though I didn't like the job, it pushed me in ways I never thought existed. After three weeks on the phones, they moved me to a sales support position."

"Now that sounds more like you, Vanessa," Dianne says.

"That's what I thought. So I was a bit surprised when I didn't pick it up as easily as I had anticipated. Though I really enjoyed interacting with the sales team and seeing the whole sales process, there was just something missing. I was intrigued with the sales position and might seek out some intentional involvement around sales, but this position didn't seem to fit."

"So, which was your favorite?" Mr. Simms asks.

"My last segment was in customer service. That's where I think I found my calling."

"Customer service?" Mr. Simms asks, a curious look on his face.

"No, Mr. Simms. Training. In preparation for the position, they had me sit through a two-day training class for new customer service representatives."

"Ah! A training class!"

"Yes. Though I wasn't conducting the training, I had a great time. Mr. Simms, I could actually see myself conducting the class."

"Good. Visualization is important."

"I knew the instructor did an excellent job because I felt totally prepared when I started the new position. Though I wouldn't want to do customer support for a living, I did very well. What's neat is that I bumped into Chaz, the instructor, about ten days later and thanked him for the training. I mentioned that he did a great job, and I asked if I could grab lunch with him and pick his brain about the training position. With permission from my manager, I spent over an hour hearing how he got into the position, what he studied in college, and what has been most and least helpful in his career. It was amazing!"

"Now that's networking in action. What's next?"

"I asked him at the end of the summer if I could shadow him for a few weeks during Christmas break, and he said I could. He mentioned that his department is often short-staffed since most people take off for the holidays and that he might be able to offer me something more than just shadowing. Can you believe it?"

"Sounds like your free internship really paid off. I'm really pleased that you didn't just punch the clock each day but really tried to get the most out of your experience. Great job."

"Guys, I'll stop back later on in the week. It's been great catching up. Oh, by the way," Vanessa reaches into her folder and pulls out two sheets of paper, "this is a copy of my end of summer review. I thought you might like to see it."

Grinning, Vanessa turns and heads out the door.

Mr. Simms skims through the review.

"Well, what does it say?" Dianne asks. "By the smile on your face, I guess it's all good? I'm so proud of her."

"I guess my job is almost done here," Mr. Simms says triumphantly.

CHAPTER 16

Don't Jump without a Net
How to Develop a Real Network

*"The way of the world is meeting people
through other people."*

Robert Kerrigan

You can see it in your mind's eye, can't you? The fire is raging, and there you are on the third floor standing on the ledge. You are being forced to make a decision, and it appears to be an ugly one. Either you go back inside and try to dance your way among the flames to the bottom floor—or you jump. The crowd is yelling for you to jump, but that decision will certainly not end well. You hear the feedback screech as the Fire Chief announces over his bullhorn, "You must jump!"

You figured that much, but every muscle refuses to move. Then you hear the screech of the bullhorn again. "Just give us thirty more seconds until we set up the net." You can't believe your ears. Wow. What a blessing. With the net set up, and the crowd bidding you to jump, you let go, knowing that this will turn out OK.

Certainly jumping with a net is good advice. And, in the above scenario, it's a necessity. Jumping into the job market without a net is equally unwise. Of course, your life is not at stake, but your sanity might be. So what type of net am I hinting at?

Have you been building your network? Most of you may think, *Yeah. I have a network. At last count, I had over 500 friends on Facebook and lots of other connections through social media.* Some might call these networks, but how many of those connections are true connections: people whom you know and who really know you? I'm afraid if you jump into this net, it will fail. You need one that is more secure: one that is built with strength and is made to endure.

What amazes me most about today is that through services like Facebook, texting, Linked-in, MySpace, and Skype, we are the most connected society in the world. Yet, we are quite unconnected. Most students spend four years building networks and connecting, yet have a hard time transferring those skills and connections out into the marketplace.

Networking is one of the most valuable skills you can acquire. If you master this skill, you'll have a much easier time finding and obtaining that job you have been hoping for. Remember, I suggested that you take notes and keep track of the people you interviewed. Well, that list really comes in handy when you are building your network. Networking, defined by Len Garille, my mentor and first boss, is going from the known to the unknown. In other words, it is having the people you know transfer the relationship they have with you to someone else.

What does going from the known to the unknown look like? For example, you want to connect with Lynne, the sales manager at Acme, but you don't know anyone there. You discover that your neighbor's son, Tom, works at Acme. Go from the known (the neighbor you know) to the unknown (her son, Tom). The key to this process is having your neighbor call Tom to let him know that her *friend* will be calling him (transferring her relationship with you to Tom) and could he please help you. Because she has placed the call, you are no longer a stranger calling, but an acquaintance. Tom will treat you in a much warmer manner than if your neighbor had just given you the number and said, "Call Tom, maybe he can help." If someone does give you a name and number to call be thankful and ask if they wouldn't mind first placing a call on your behalf. That little step can make a huge difference.

You are no longer a stranger calling, but an acquaintance.

Once you have connected with Tom, there is a good chance you'll have a pleasant conversation about how you know his mom, what you studied, and what you want to do. You'll also talk about what he does at Acme. At some point, he may ask, "How can I help?"

You have the opportunity of asking for one or two favors. The first is to conduct an informational interview over a cup of coffee, and the second is to go from the known (Tom) to the unknown (a connection of his inside the company such as Lynne). Tom may not be the best person in the company to help you get to where you want to go, but my guess is that he knows who can. Ask if he could please place a personal call to Lynne in sales and let her know that you'll be calling. Again, when you call Lynne, you will not be a stranger but a 'friend' of Tom's.

Begin to build your contact, a.k.a 'known' list. Who do you know? Who are you friends with? Who can you pick up the phone and call, text, or email? Try to expand this list. Have you included professors, teaching assistants, alumni, parents of friends, and neighbors? Almost all those people have family members as well, many of whom work at companies and in industries that intersect or intimately interact with your interests and goals.

In general, people enjoy helping people. Start with the premise that if you ask, they will help, and you will meet new people and find opportunities you never knew existed.

One of the most effective opportunities you have for networking is so close you can touch it: alumni. If you have declared a major, you are part of a unique group of people who have graduated from the same college or university. As soon as you declare a major, you should begin contacting alumni. Continue to contact three to five alumni each semester. The first reason you'll want to reach out to this amazing resource is to perform a simple informational interview to learn about them. (See questions at the end of the chapter.) The second reason you'll want to contact them is to build your list. Many of the alumni have landed in industries that will interest you, so now you have a 'known' on the inside. If you start this process the first semester of your sophomore year, by the time you graduate, you will have over thirty fledgling relationships with professionals who are on the inside of industry.

To take your alumni contact list to the next level, after your initial connection, ask if it would be all right to reach out to them once a semester just to keep in touch. What you are doing here is asking them for permission to contact them. Once you have permission, make it a point to contact them at least once per semester to see how they are doing, what they are learning, or special projects they are on. These alumni may also be great contacts for group projects or class research.

Building your network is about meeting people and having a genuine interest in them. This is much different from 'Linking-in' with them or 'friend requesting' them. This is getting to know someone, listening to what he or she does, and forming a friendship. If you ask most people where they went to school, studied, and are working, they will usually reciprocate by asking you similar questions. If there is a connection, don't be shy about asking if you could give them a call because you are interested in learning more about what they do or where they work. Then ask for a business card. What will you give them? A post-it note or cocktail napkin with your contact info scribbled on it? Instead, have a simple business card with your contact information, major, and graduation date printed on it. It is a very inexpensive way to look professional.

Work on your networking skills. Don't let your online connections give you a false sense of accomplishment. Online connections are generally not as powerful as personal connections.

If you've been following the tips throughout this book, you are already busy with a purpose. When you are busy with a purpose, it means that you are involved in different activities, clubs, jobs, classes, and organizations. This means you are coming in contact with many great people. All these contacts are opportunities for deeper networking. I've heard it said, and I believe it to be true, that the best jobs are often landed by personal recommendations and connections. Those occur because of networking.

Setting Up Your Network:

1. **Now that you have claimed a major, contact three to five alumni each semester:**
    *   Return to career services or your faculty advisor and see if you can get the contact information for three to five alumni who graduated from your major and who are working.
    *   Reach out to each of the alumni and begin forming a relationship with them.
        *   If you want to get the most out of this experience, avoid using this as an opportunity to ask for a job. If alumni sense that you're calling looking for a job, it may hamper any success in developing a real relationship.
    *   Ask what they would do differently if they had to do it again?
    *   Which classes did they find most/least helpful? Which classes were most/least relevant? Who was their favorite professor? What advice might they have for you?
    *   Keep in touch with each contact with one or two quick emails per semester.
    *   In your junior or senior year, ask if you could job shadow.
    *   Try to form an informal mentor relationship. These 'knowns' are a great resource.
    *   If these alumni are not working in an environment that interests you, they may know someone who is. Ask to be introduced.

2. **Each personal interview performed in Chapter 11: Listening for the Outward Call should be valued as a networking opportunity.**
    *   After each interview, record the person's name, the company for whom they work, and contact information.
    *   Send a thank-you note and a business card along with a statement that you hope you can contact them again if you have further questions. This leaves the door open to reconnect, even years from now.

- Stay in touch with these new connections and foster them. From time to time, reach out and let them know what you are doing.
- Not only will these interviews help shape your views and opinions, they are the beginning of a professional network.

3. **What extracurricular activities, groups, or clubs are you involved in?**
   - Seek school functions, sports clubs, church groups, humanitarian agencies, business associations, community organizations, and student activities to get involved with.
   - If you belong and are active in any of these, you already possess a network. Now these relationships and your network must be cultivated.

4. **Business Cards**
   - These can be very inexpensive, even free at certain sites, (e.g., vistaprint.com).
   - Keep them simple. Avoid bold and/or distracting colors.
   - Keep fonts legible.
   - Contact information should be up-to-date and professional. Avoid email addresses like "Kegman23@univ.edu."
   - Be careful about placing personal addresses on cards; you may just want to put the town and state.
   - If you are including a cell phone number, make sure your cell phone message is professional. I've heard some doozies!

Case Study
Vanessa's Résumé

"Vanessa, I have one last assignment. Follow me into the conference room." Mr. Simms pulls out her file. "Remember when we first met, I asked you for your résumé?"

"Yeah, my anxiety went through the roof. I didn't even know what I wanted to study."

"I think you've done a great job, Vanessa."

"Great job, Mr. Simms? Doing what?"

"You've done a great job writing your résumé."

"Mr. Simms, you may have misunderstood me. I still don't have a résumé."

"Yes, you do. You've been busy writing one."

"Mr. Simms?"

"Vanessa, what students fail to recognize is that a résumé is a reflection of themselves. The résumé is the result of the discovery process. The work you've done looking back at your experiences and creating new experiences have resulted in a fantastic résumé." Mr. Simms pauses to let his words sink in. "What kind of information does a résumé contain?"

"I've never sat down to write one, but I've seen a few. I seem to remember that they had the person's name, contact information, and schooling."

I'll bet you didn't know that you spelled résumé with an A, E, I, O and U?

"You certainly have that information. What else does a résumé contain?"

"I remember seeing a section titled Objectives. I think that is where I'd indicate what I'd like to do for a career."

"Vanessa, how does one know what she wants to do for a career?"

There is a long pause as Vanessa nervously spins her pen on the table. "I guess she could write an objective based on whatever job she is applying for."

"Whatever job? Vanessa, think about our time together last semester. What did we talk about?"

Vanessa's face lights up. "Ice cream," she says.

"Yes. Ice cream."

"We figured out our favorite flavors through the discovery process."

"Where does the discovery process appear on a résumé?"

Vanessa starts to speak, pauses, and then smiles. "The experiences, paid and unpaid, appear on our résumé. Those experiences should reflect or support our objective. Right?"

"I do now. My experiences, past and present, give a voice to my inward and outward call. Those experiences support my career objective."

"As I was saying, you've done a great job writing your résumé. But you are not done. Continue excelling in your classwork and seek out additional experiences that will further confirm your interests and calling: experiences that will help support your career objective."

"Mr. Simms, I think being an RA and working as a campus tour guide this year are going to be a big help in the confirmation process."

"Vanessa, at times I've used legal language when describing the discovery process. We spent a lot of time in discovery, which is where you pour yourself into the gathering of facts and evidence."

"This is where cases are won and lost if I remember correctly. That is where I was busy with a purpose."

"Exactly. When a legal team is done gathering its evidence, it begins to hone in on its strongest pieces of evidence. Then the team begins to build its case."

"For me, that period of focus would be my intentional involvement. Right?"

"Right. Then the legal team presents its case. If it has done a great job, the verdict should be self-evident. Vanessa, your résumé is your closing argument. When a recruiter looks over your résumé and compares it with the job description for which you are applying, there should be enough evidence presented for him to interview you. Your interview is now an opportunity to expound on how the discovery process has led you to this interview and why this job is right for you."

Vanessa sits for a minute to absorb what she's just heard. She looks up and smiles. "Mr. Simms, how did you do it?"

"Do what, Vanessa?"

"I remember walking in here last semester terrified at the prospect of one day interviewing. I know I still have work to do, but I can't wait to tell my story."

"Vanessa, you are going to have a great story to tell. But I need to correct you. I didn't do it. You did it. Remember, when we first met

I shared with you that you'd be doing the heavy lifting. I just told you what to lift."

"And, boy, am I sore." Vanessa rubs her arms.

"Well, Counsel, are you ready to present your closing arguments?"

Vanessa clears her throat. "If it would please the Court, I would like to address the jury with my closing argument." She stands up, walks to the door, and then stops and turns to Mr. Simms. "Your student helper is graduating in December; do you have someone to take her place? I'd like to work here in career services. I can totally see myself teaching the classes she's conducting."

"Do you have any references?" Mr. Simms jokes. "Dianne and I were wondering when you were going to ask. Let's talk more about that next week." Mr. Simms stands up. "My nine o'clock is here."

As they exit the room, Dianne announces, "Patrick, Mr. Simms will see you now."

Mr. Simms waves to Vanessa. "See you next week." Then he turns toward Patrick.

"He'd like to learn about writing a résumé," Dianne says.

Vanessa and Mr. Simms exchange a smile. "Patrick," Mr. Simms says, "did you know 'résumé' was spelled with an A, E, I, O and a U?"

"Sir?"

The Discovery Worksheet

Take note: (E) = Experience, (I) = Inward call, (O) = Outward call

High School Years:

Academics: The High School Years

- Review your high school transcript. (E,I)
- Which classes did you really enjoy and/or did well in and why? (E,I)
- Talk to your teachers. How would they evaluate your performance? (O)
- Did you and/or others notice you had a natural ability or affinity in certain subjects? (I,O)
- Why did you enjoy these subjects? (E.g., Was it the subject, teacher, or social environment of the class?) (I)

1. _____
2. _____
3. _____
4. _____
5. _____
6. _____

- Which classes did you not enjoy or do well in and why? (I)
- Did your teachers agree? (O)
- Here you want to explore the lack of affinity or gifts you have in certain subjects. (I)

1. _____
2. _____
3. _____
4. _____
5. _____
6. _____

Extracurricular Activities: The High School Years

- Record below *every* extracurricular activity in which you partic-ipated: during school and after school. (E.g., choir, sports, plays, debate team, mission trips, volunteer positions, homecoming committee.) (E)
- What did you like/dislike about each? (I) Did you or others notice a talent, skill, or ability that stood out? (I,O)
- Did you see yourself gravitating toward or avoiding similar posi-tions and activities? (I)
- What did you learn in each position? (E,I)
- For example: Choir – I really enjoyed choir, I sang all four years. I learned how to work in a group, and gained the confidence to perform solos. I overcame the fear of singing in front of groups, and now I love performing for people.

1. _____
2. _____
3. _____
4. _____
5. _____
6. _____

Work Experience: The High School Years

- Which jobs have you held? (E)
- What skills did you learn in each position? (E,I)
- Did you enjoy the learning experience? (I)
- Did you perform well? (I)
- What talents did you discover or excel in? (E)
- How did your employer rate your performance? (O)
- Did your employer notice or comment on a skill or ability you displayed? (O)
- Did you have a formal review? What were the results? (O)

1. _____
2. _____
3. _____
4. _____

5. _____
6. _____

College Years:

<u>Academics</u>: The College Years

- Review your YTD transcript. (E,I)
- Which classes did you really enjoy and/or did well in and why? (E,I)
- Talk to your teachers. How would they evaluate your performance? (O)
- Did you notice, or did others notice a natural ability or affinity in certain subjects? (I,O)
- Why did you enjoy these subjects? (E.g., Was it the subject, teacher, or social element of the class?) (I)

1. _____
2. _____
3. _____
4. _____
5. _____
6. _____

- Which classes did you not enjoy or not do well in? Why? (I)
- Did your teachers agree? (O)
- Here you want to explore the lack of affinity or gifts you have in certain subjects. (I)

1. _____
2. _____
3. _____
4. _____
5. _____
6. _____

Extracurricular Activities: The College Years

- Record below *every* extra curricular activity in which you participated: during school and after school (e.g., choir, sports, plays, debate team, mission trips, volunteer positions, homecoming committee). (E)
- What did you like/dislike about each? (I) Did you or others notice a talent, skill, or ability that stood out? (I,O)
- Did you see yourself gravitating toward or avoiding similar positions and activities? (I)
- What did you learn in each position? (E,I)

1. _____
2. _____
3. _____
4. _____
5. _____
6. _____

Work Experience: The College Years

- Which jobs have you held? (E)
- What skills did you learn in each position? (E, I)
- Did you enjoy the learning experience? (I)
- Did you perform well? (I)
- What talents did you discover or excel in? (E)
- How did your employer rate your performance? (O)
- Did they notice or comment on a skill or ability you displayed? (O)
- Did you have a formal review? What were the results? (O)

1. _____
2. _____
3. _____
4. _____
5. _____
6. _____

Acknowledgements:

The great success of *Hire on a WHIM* was both humbling and enticing. Humbling because I am still amazed at the impact and feedback I receive from those who have read it. Enticing because I still have more to say, and so I continue to write.

The foundation for my philosophies found in *'Right'* began with a conversation between my good friend Bill Kessler and I back in 1995. I've applied the concepts of the inward and outward call when I manage, parent, and coach.

I'd like to thank the many people who have weighed in on this project in its many forms.

A special thanks to my brother Victor who stepped in as my content editor. He helped smooth out rough patches and helped the flow and logic. It is a better book because of him.

My editor, Marilyn Gasior Ed.D. who showed saint-like patience as she polished my writing.

I'm also very grateful to have met Amanda Martin while she was interning as an editor at a local publishing company. She offered valuable insights and edits. Though just out of college, she is well on her way to completing the AEIOU formula for success.

Thanks to Adele Annisi, a terrific friend and editor who helped with the earliest version. To Ron Pearce, Megan Montgomery, and Noel Leuzarder who read *'Right'* in its most crude form; someone had to be first.

Many friends and professionals took time to read and comment on the book as it matured. I am grateful to each who has played a role in *'Rights'* final product. Thanks to my awesome wife Paula and to Ione Prawius, Charlie Smith, Chris Wagner, Deanna Cuomo, Diane Faust, Beth Biesley, Peter Ferrigno, George Fisher, Chuck Sutton, Evan Showell, and my father, Victor Miller.

I'm amazed that such terrific professionals have come across my path. Again I thank the team at Career Services, Grove City College: Jim Thrasher, Mandy Sposato, and Erica Mayer. You all have been a great support and source of inspiration to me and my subject matter.

I'm grateful for the support and insights Shari Goldstein and Dr. Ingrid Johanson from Florida Atlantic University provided.

Thanks to the students who read and provided insightful feedback: Faith Leuzarder, Caleb Thrasher, Ben Hagan, Marshal Cuomo, Ciara Picciano, Andrew Wagner, Britney Rhodes, and (at the time) MBA candidate Noel Leuzarder.

About the Author

Garrett Miller is the founder and president of CoTria, a productivity training company.

He graduated from the University of Rhode Island and worked for a Fortune 40 company for eighteen years, the last ten as a manager. After an award-winning career, Garrett began his latest venture as business owner, author, keynote speaker, coach, and trainer. CoTria's clients include some of the world's greatest companies. Garrett has been married nineteen years to his amazing wife Paula and is the proud father of three.

Additional Resources from the Author

Books: *Hire on a WHIM – The Four Qualities that Make for Great Employees* (Dog Ear Press 2010)

CoTria: A Productivity Training Company:
Garrett is the founder and president of CoTria. Garrett began CoTria in 2007 and has helped some of the world's greatest organizations become more efficient by Creating Space in their days so that they can get more done. The Creating Space workshops are fun, interactive, and guaranteed to help attendees recapture valuable time. The average attendee recaptures 10-15 days per year. The Creating Space workshops help organizations save time by mastering their technology and by changing behavior so that the results have lasting impact.

Creating Space Workshops:

- Hire on WHIM - A one-day workshop designed to help hiring managers learn a simple and repeatable formula for making excellent hiring decisions.
- Creating Space with Outlook® - Learn tips and tricks to help you master this amazing productivity tool so you can save time and boost your productivity.
- Creating Space with BlackBerry® - Turn your BlackBerry into an indispensable productivity tool. Learn tips and tricks to increase your productivity.
- Creating Space by Managing Time - Learn how to say *yes* to success and *no* to distractions that pull you away from your priorities.
- Creating Space with the iPad/iPhone - Learn tips and tricks to help you save time and boost your productivity.

- <u>Get Control of Email®</u> - Spend less time in your inbox. Learn to manage your inbox, write clear and concise communications, send less, and get less email.
- <u>Get Control, Get Organized®</u> - Get your information organized once and for all. Develop a phenomenal filing system so that you never lose an electronic file again.
- <u>Get Control of Meetings®</u> - Learn to have less meetings, shorter meetings, and more productive meetings.

Garrett is available for keynote speeches and corporate training.

Visit: <u>www.cotria.com</u>
<u>www.hireonawhim.com</u>
<u>www.hired-right.com</u>